Ruth,
Aloha + Good Health,
Grady

Dr. Deal's
⋝ DELICIOUS ⋜
DETOX DIET
WEIGHT LOSS
WELLNESS LIFESTYLE

By

DR. GRADY A. DEAL, Ph.D., D.C.

D1564033

Published By:

LIVING WELLNESS
P.O. Box 279
Koloa, Kauai, Hawaii 96756
(800) 338-6977

DR. DEAL'S DELICIOUS DETOX DIET
WEIGHT LOSS
WELLNESS LIFESTYLE

DISCLAIMER: This book is for education only and not intended to provide professional advice. Consult a nutritionally oriented doctor for medical or psychological diagnosis and treatment.

Caricature By
EDGAR K. GUTHRIE
For your own caricature from a photo, write or call:
2444 Hihiwai St., Apt. 703
Honolulu, Hawaii 96826
(808) 955-2644

Published By:
LIVING WELLNESS
P.O. Box 279
Koloa, Kauai, Hawaii 96756
(800) 338-6977

Printed in the United States of America

DEDICATED TO

ROBERLEIGH
My Beloved Wife

"People are no longer satisfied just dealing with symptoms and superficial evaluations, they want to dig down and get to the root cause of problems."
— *Roberleigh Deal*

CONTENTS

FOREWORD

Although I have been asked to write forewords to quite a few books during the past forty years, and I have been asked to introduce speakers at gatherings in many parts of the world, the task of adequately introducing Dr. Grady Deal and his ground-breaking work in the field of health is my most formidable task. It is formidable because I need to convince you, in a few words, of the vital necessity of your heeding his recommendations as presented in this work. I need to let you know how exciting and fulfilling your life can become simply by adapting or giving up your present lifestyle and by entering into a new world of healthful vitality. Fortunately for this task, I can endorse Dr. Deal's work because I have been the beneficiary of his healthy routine at a time of my life when most men my age are trying to find a suitable nursing home, if they are not already in the cemetery and receiving weekly visitations from their widows. I can confidently look forward to three decades past the biblical seventy years, decades during which I can continue my researches, my writings, and my lectures, simply because I have finally become informed about the most important subject of all, how to maintain a daily regimen which keeps me fit.

During my first sixty years, I engorged a daily diet of meat three times a day, rich desserts and vegetables boiled in city water which was heavily laced with chlorine, sodium fluoride and other poisons sold to your ignorant city fathers by the drug trust. Over a half century of this abuse left me with puffy yellow eyes, heavily stained teeth, and a prematurely aged physique which now required that I nap at least an hour each afternoon, like a baby. By following Dr. Deal's treatment and recommended dietary changes, I turned this situation around, saving my body from the diabetes, strokes, heart attacks, and Alzheimer's disease which are routine occurrences for persons in my age group. One phrase alone is worth the price of the book — no dairy. However, I urge you not to stop there, but to adopt Dr. Deal's entire health program of correct nutrition, treatments and exercise which will enable you to double your productivity and to enjoy each day in a manner which you believed was no longer possible.

— Eustace Mullins
1991

INTRODUCTION

Dr. Deal's Delicious Detox Diet & Wellness Lifestyle introduces a cleansing detoxification diet of whole grains, lentils, beans, seeds, nuts, vegetables, sprouts, fruit, fish and eggs; natural therapies to treat underlying metabolic imbalances and other health problems; and encouragement to help you overcome any psychological resistance to wellness.

The Detox Diet is a permanent, clean diet designed to rest, fast, cleanse, detoxify and nurture the body every day. The recommended foods are non-toxic, clean foods to clean out the accumulated toxins in the body left from previous diets. These wholesome foods are easy to digest and eliminate thereby giving the body a rest and a chance to heal while at the same time providing all the most important nutrients to make you strong and healthy, perhaps more healthy than you have ever been in your life.

You may want a good Detox Diet & Wellness Lifestyle because toxicity from unhealthful foods, bad habits, untreated metabolic disorders and medical drugs causes systemic toxicity, free radical pathology, inflammation, swelling, edema, nerve irritation, muscle contractions, pain, degeneration, disease, premature aging and an early death.

Detoxification is simply removing the toxins and poisons from your cells, tissues, skin, organs and glands by eliminating toxic foods and bad habits; by correcting metabolic functions in the body with herbs, enzymes, glandulars and other natural therapies to speed detoxification and healing; by building up the immune system responsible for keeping germs, viruses, parasites, macromolecules, foreign proteins, allergens, non-human antibodies and other injurious elements out of the body and also cleaning up these toxins which have already entered the blood, lymph, cells, tissues, organs and glands; and by exercising the body regularly to get the toxins moving and out of the body.

Prevent further toxic insult by excluding toxic foods and substances, free oils (any processed oil removed from its source), dairy, sugar, soft drinks, pork, chemically contaminated meat or fowl, fast foods, alcohol, smoking, street drugs, medical drugs and other poisonous materials unfortunately found in the average

American diet and lifestyle.

Detoxify and build up your body by correcting the basic metabolic processes involved in digestion and assimilation of nutrients, elimination of wastes, and rebuilding, repairing and healing the body. If your metabolic functions are imbalanced, blocked or worn-out, you cannot digest food or assimilate its nutrients; you cannot properly eliminate dietary and metabolic toxic wastes which tend to accumulate in the body; and your body will degenerate, suffer from chronic infections and fail to heal effectively and timely.

Thyroid metabolism, for example, is one of the basic metabolic processes that governs the metabolic rate for all functions of the body and if your thyroid hormones are low, all cell, tissue, organ, gland and metabolic functions are abnormal and any detoxification and wellness program will ultimately fail until thyroid dysfunction is corrected. Hypothyroidism or low thyroid function causes a drop in the normal body temperature and inhibits the production of red and white blood cells in the bone marrow which decreases red blood cell oxygen transport to the body for food metabolism, energy and heat and decreases white blood cell activity in fighting off colds, flu, sinusitis, sore throats, candidiasis and other infections. Hypothyroidism can also cause fatigue, depression, weight gain, etc. and can cause liver sluggishness, decreased blood circulation and poor oxygen/waste exchange which slow down the detoxification process and cause systemic toxicity.

Proper detoxification and healing the body are also limited by hiatal hernia which interferes with the vagus nerve supply to all the organs and glands in the body and disrupts their metabolic functions, one of which is decreased hydrochloric stomach acid output which decreases digestion, limits hydrochloric acid's killing power of germs and viruses and can increase infection all over the body.

Candidiasis, another underlying metabolic disorder, toxifies the body and damages the immune system. Millions of candida organisms excrete toxic wastes during their short lifetime and when they die, their body parts poison the large intestine, which in turn poisons the whole body because intestinal toxins readily pass through the colon wall (leaky gut syndrome) and are carried throughout the body.

Leaky gut syndrome poisons the liver and the entire body.

Large intestine toxins and germs from unhealthful foods, bad habits, processed food chemicals, herbicides, pesticides, candidiasis, constipation, etc. wear out and break down the colon wall immune system allowing these toxins to easily pass through the colon wall. The lymph vessels and the hepatic vein pick up and carry these toxins, germs, feces, macromolecules, allergens and foreign invaders to the lymph nodes and liver for detoxification. But the lymph nodes and liver too are soon worn out and overwhelmed by so many toxins and allow these noxious elements to be carried to every cell in the body, from head to toe, causing systemic toxicity, inflammation, swelling, edema, degeneration, disease and delayed detoxification and healing times. Injuries never heal properly; chronic infection lurks just beneath the surface all your life.

Little or no exercise to speak of causes blood and lymph stasis and toxicity. Exercise increases blood and lymph circulation carrying nutrients to the cells and waste products away from the cells.

Hypothyroidism, hiatal hernia, low hydrochloric stomach acid output, candidiasis, leaky gut syndrome are some of the important underlying metabolic disorders which need attention. Others are systemic toxicity, free radical pathology, constipation, parasites, chronic Epstein-Barr virus and hypoglycemia. All of these underlying metabolic problems may need treatment with natural therapies as part of a complete detoxification and wellness program. Eat clean, natural foods and eliminate unhealthful foods and bad habits which poison our bodies. You are also encouraged to exercise.

The Detox Diet & Wellness Lifestyle understandably emphasizes detoxification because any diet or healing program is incomplete without detoxification. The Detox Diet itself detoxifies the body; eliminating unhealthful foods and bad habits detoxifies the body; correcting underlying metabolic disorders detoxifies the body; chiropractic adjustment help detoxify the body, exercise detoxifies the body; building up the immune system detoxifies the body; and loving comfort and raising the human spirit sparks the will to detoxify and heal the body.

Given half a chance, the eliminative organs partially detoxify the body if not constantly overworked, congested and inflamed by more toxins from an unhealthful lifestyle. Waste materials are released from the body via the urine from the kidneys, via the expiration from the lungs, via the sweat from the skin; via the mucus and discharges from the sinuses, lungs and gastrointestinal tract; via the feces from the colon. Wastes and toxins are also released via alternate vicarious pathways in the form of discharges from the male or female breasts, prostate or ovaries-uterus-vagina when the regular eliminative channels are overloaded with toxins causing the present epidemic of disease and cancer of the breasts, prostate and ovaries-uterus-vagina according to Dr. Henry Bieler, M.D. Note, however, that toxic release from the eliminative organs is never a clean sweep; toxic residues, especially excess toxins, are routinely stored in every cell in your body.

Detoxifying the body builds up the immune system and stimulates the healing process. Once dietary, lifestyle and metabolic toxins are in general circulation, the macrophages, phagocytes, T-killer cells, B-cells, T-helper, T-suppressor cells, T-memory cells, lymphocytes and antibodies of the immune system in the blood, lymph and tissues ingest, clean up and detoxify the toxins throughout the body. Therefore, detoxifying the body with a Detox Diet, eliminating unhealthful foods and bad habits and correcting underlying metabolic disorders will decrease the amount of toxic assault on the immune system and give it a rest and a boost and also will give your body a chance to rest and heal.

It is fair to say that most diseases, such as cancer, arthritis and other degenerative diseases, are caused by a weak or suppressed immune system, which means the immune system must be stimulated and supported to overcome the illness. It is also fair to say that toxicity from an unhealthful lifestyle suppresses the immune system initially in the first place and that the immune system can never be fully brought back to optimal efficiency unless the body is first detoxified. In short, dietary and lifestyle related toxicity calls the immune system into play to clean up the toxins; and you cannot rebuild the immune system and regain your health until you clean up the toxins with a good program of detoxification and healing.

Learning about and following through with a Detox Diet, detoxification and healing program depends upon eliminating any resistance to wholesome food, natural therapies and wellness. Individual resistance may be around the issues: not wanting to give up favorite foods or bad habits; staying unhealthy to avoid responsibility in relationships and work; using bad health to punish self and others; preferring easy and quick orthodox drugs, surgery and radiation therapies instead of the hassle of adopting a healthful lifestyle and using natural therapies; siding with orthodox medicine to appear superior to alternative health nuts; being weak and undisciplined; giving up hope and throwing in the towel on life as a result of personal trauma, real or imagined; being passive-dependent (asking for help and then doing nothing to help self) or hostile-dependent (asking for help and then fighting tooth and nail to sabotage positive action); being unloving, angry or unforgiving; worrying self to death; procrastinating or being lazy; feeling sorry for yourself; reinforcing personal, emotional and physical problems with symptomatic drugs, oftentimes useless talk therapy, complaining, manipulating, sabotaging, etc. instead of releasing all probems to God; going to orthodox doctors who let you get away with murder and avoid going to alternative doctors who are likely to confront you about unhealthful foods, bad habits and a negative orientation to wellness and life; not being ready to get well or improve diet and spiritual life; etc.

The orthodox medical monopoly has a tragic record of blocking wellness, in that, the United States despite claims to the contrary is one of the sickest nations in the world with most of the population trusting their Establishment doctors and consequently suffering and dying from unnecessary cardiovascular disease, cancer and other degenerative diseases directly caused by the diet, processed foods, unproven medical drugs, surgery and radiation recommended by orthodox medical doctors, osteopaths, nurses, registered dietitians, medical associations, health charities, federal, state and local government health bureaus, health insurance companies, medical drug companies, the processed food industry and the controlled media — all manipulated from behind the scenes by the financial elite and a vast army of good ol' boys to sell unproven, toxic medical drugs and devitalized processed foods for profit to keep us sick and dependent on them to control and enslave us more easily.

The medical Establishment makes and keeps us sick and dependent as follows: the germ and chemical imbalance theories are self-serving rationalizations to justify selling antibiotics and other drugs to enrich the medical drug and processed food industry; actual state laws in all fifty states demand that unproven, toxic medical

drugs are the treatment of first choice for every disease regardless
if they cure or cause disease as a pay-back from the medical drug
industry's annual bribes to medical schools and researchers to do
drug research, mostly fabricated or not properly scientifically
validated to ''prove'' that drugs are safe and effective as a front
to sell more drugs; over 90% of all prescribed and over-the-counter
medical drugs have NEVER been scientifically tested on humans
with both a control group and an experimental group to determine
the drugs' safety and effectiveness; most medical drugs are
inadequately tested in so-called clinical trials without controls on
college students, people in old age homes and prison inmates and
animal studies which do not meet the minimum standards of scientific research, not by any stretch of the imagination; our government's own research found that only 3% of all medical drugs have
important potential, that the average new ''wonder'' drug is on
the market on the average for only five years after which it is
rightfully (but too late) declared too toxic and ineffective for use,
only to be replaced with another not so ''new'' wonder drug with
the same problems of toxicity and uselessness; psychiatric and anti-
depressant drugs often make the emotional or mental disorder worse
in the long run; a survey of all research regarding the effectiveness
of psychotherapy consistently shows that talk therapy is unproven
and ineffective, that lay persons are just as effective as profes-
sionals, that patients on a waiting list to be seen for psychotherapy
recovered at the same rate as those actually seen for counseling
and that psychotherapy can cause dependency and emotional
instability later in life; medical testing is often invalid or inaccurate
half the time; up to 80% of the most common surgeries are
unnecessary; the inference that any alternative doctor who provides
unproven therapies, makes wide claims to their effectiveness and
makes a big profit is a quack falls back in the face of orthodox
medical doctors as suggested by Dr. Robert Mendelsohn, M.D.
in *How to Raise a Healthy Child in Spite of Your Doctor* by his
statement, ''That sounds like modern medicine to me''; modern
medicine has failed in that cancer deaths have increased 600% in
the last 20 years killing 1 in 3 persons, cardiovascular disease
continues to be the leading cause of disease for 1 out of 2 people,
and 1 in 5 people have a mental illness (often caused by doctors
in the first place) requiring medical treatment, which is ineffective and counterproductive; all underlying metabolic disorders,

such as systemic toxicity, free radical pathology, constipation, candidiasis, parasites, chronic Epstein-Barr virus, hiatal hernia, hypothyroidism, hypoglycemia, etc. are routinely ignored, misdiagnosed, mistreated and ridiculed as quack theories but which in reality, are the most important causes of disease; ''our'' government will remove the medical license of any doctor who treats disease with natural therapies and refuses to push drugs as the treatment of first choice, as dictated by the drug industry; to protect its monopoly, the medical Establishment puts down chiropractors and naturopaths as not being real doctors, not scientifically trained and not recognized by the American Medical Association when in fact, chiropractors and naturopaths have the same pre-medical college training as medical students, their schools have the same science curriculum (physiology, anatomy, chemistry, pathology but not drugs and surgery) as medical schools, chiropractors and naturopaths are regulated by their own national and state associations and why would any honest, good doctor want to be recognized and approved by the American Medical Association, which was called the American Murder Association by a group of dissident medical doctors during one of its annual meetings.

Glad to get that out of the way. You can read more about the ineffectiveness and dangers of modern medicine by reading the recommended books listed in the last chapter.

You can understand and appreciate a good health program more completely by ranking its solutions and causes, beginning with the most important first, as follows.

- **Overcoming Individual and Medical Monopoly Resistance**
  Unity with God or alienation from God
  Loving and compassionate or unloving and cold
  Forgiving and charitable or unforgiving and envious
  Good or bad relations with spouse, family, friends
  Release problems to God or reinforce them with talk
  Open or resistive to a Detox Diet & Wellness Program
  Honest or corrupt doctors, bureaucrats and charities

- **Choosing Natural or Orthodox Healing**
  Healthful diet and habits or unhealthful diet and habits
  Natural therapies or toxic drugs, surgery, radiation
  Detoxification or toxicity and free radical pathology
  Colon cleansing or colon and tissue constipation

Corrects or worsens underlying metabolic disorders
Exercise or sedentary

- **Rebuilding or Tearing Down Immune System**
  Strengthening or weakening immune system
  Natural immune boosters or drug immune blockers

Each step of the detoxification and healing process is important and some are more important than others and all together constitute a complete program. Determine where you are in your life and your health program. And if you are not where you want to be, the Detox Diet, Weight Loss, Wellness Lifestyle can help you get more healthy, fit and slim and help you feel and look great.

The chapters are arranged alphabetically for your convenience.

ALLERGY ADDICTION TO FAVORITE FOODS

Why do I feel terrible? It may be a food allergy-addiction. Allergy-addiction, much like systemic toxicity, candidiasis, chronic Epstein-Barr virus, parasites and hypothyroidism, can cause almost any physical, emotional or mental problem including runny nose, sneezing, headache, chronic fatigue, indigestion, gas, bedwetting, dark circles and puffiness under the eyes, swollen glands, fluid retention, neck and back problems, frequent infections, arthritis, cardiovascular disease, cancer, irritability, insomnia, female pelvic disorders, obesity, depression, anxiety, mental illness and many more health problems.

Food allergy is often an undiagnosed underlying cause of allergy reactions to pollen, dust, animal dander and other external environmental factors. You first became allergic to certain foods which made you overly sensitive to pollen and other environmental irritants. The solution is to clear up the food allergy and any underlying candidiasis, parasites, hypothyroidism or systemic toxicity to improve or eliminate the allergy reactions to pollen, etc. All without drugs.

Food allergy-addiction is caused by: feeding babies cow's milk, meat, eggs, cereals, etc. before one year of age before they are able to digest these foods; eating the same foods too often, especially, dairy, wheat, corn, eggs, soybeans, and citrus fruits; overeating, which depletes hydrochloric acid and digestive enzymes; eating devitalized foods and thousands of chemical additives from processed foods which inflame the intestines and break down the immune system of the intestinal walls, making them porous to large altered protein molecules which pass into the bloodstream as allergy-immune complexes; undigested food particles and metabolic wastes from unhealthful foods, incomplete digestion, food chemicals, coffee, sugar, alcohol, cigarettes, street drugs, medical drugs, etc. also enter the bloodstream causing allergy reactions.

These abnormal proteins and metabolic wastes from an unhealthful diet and bad habits accumulate in the bloodstream and

1

tissues which inflame, weaken, congest, wear out and damage the joints, glands and organs, especially the digestive and eliminative organs as well as the immune system which hopelessly tries to fight off these invading toxins day after day, year after year until your body is worn out and toxic in every cell from head to toe. This is what is known as *systemic toxicity* which means your body is filled with toxins which interfere with every metabolic function in the body causing allergy and other health problems.

Repeated consumption of small or large amounts of any dairy food, for example, creates increasing amounts of dairy toxins and allergy-immune complexes. The dairy allergens or antigens stimulate the immune system to produce antibodies in response to the foreign dairy proteins. The antibodies coat the body's mucous membranes in the gastrointestinal tract as well as the sinuses, respiratory tract, skin and vagina. IgA antibodies in the intestinal walls and other mucous membranes serve as a barrier to the external world to keep undigested food molecules, altered dairy proteins in this example, and germs from being absorbed through the walls of small and large intestines into the blood and lymph system and to keep airborne chemicals, pollen and germs from being absorbed through the skin, sinuses and lungs.

Accumulating amounts of dairy allergens from repeated ingestion of dairy foods create dairy antibodies which form antibody-antigen complexes causing an allergic reaction which releases histamine, serotonin, leukotriene, kinins, prostaglandins, complement and immune complexes.

Histamine, for example, causes dilation of the blood vessels. Runny nose and hayfever symptoms are caused by histamine dilating the blood vessels of the nose and sinuses making them leak or run. Histamine-mediated dilation of blood vessels can stretch the nerves along the blood vessels causing swelling and pain. The brain may swell causing cerebral edema and can cause any neurological or emotional symptom. Large amounts of histamine from an allergic reaction to penicillin can cause anaphylactic shock and death.

Histamine can also cause involuntary smooth muscle contractions which control breathing and gastrointestinal functions. Much of gastrointestinal illness, ulcers, colitis, etc. is caused by or related to allergy. An allergy to dairy causes histamine mediated abnormal contractions of the intestines and lungs, mucus accumulation, congestion, toxicity, inflammation, breakdown of the immune system and infection.

Making matters worse and more confusing, allergy reactions to the most common allergy foods, dairy, wheat, corn, soy, etc. are masked as the body attempts to adapt to stress. When an allergy is developed to dairy, for example, the symptoms may be masked and hidden. Withdrawing from dairy by not eating it on schedule unmasks the heretofore hidden allergic reaction to dairy causing allergy symptoms similar to withdrawal from heroin.

This delayed type of allergy reaction to dairy and other allergens can be explained by the ideas of systemic toxicity, healing crisis and allergy-addiction. Food allergy is simply a special case of systemic toxicity as outlined above, i.e., dairy toxins accumulate in every cell in the body and continue to accumulate as long as the food is eaten regularly.

If dairy is not eaten on a regular timely basis or is temporarily withdrawn or if a healing crisis ensues as a result of eliminating all dairy from the diet, the dairy toxins are dumped by all the cells into the bloodstream and lymph fluid on their way out of the body. Once out of the cells and into the general circulation, the dairy toxins poison, irritate, inflame and overstimulate the tissues, glands, organs and nervous system. These withdrawal symptoms are experienced as discomfort, inflammation, swelling, edema, pain, irritability, excessive appetite, cramps, diarrhea, constipation, sleep disturbances, fatigue, manic states, anxiety, depression, paranoia, schizophrenia, etc.

The escaping dairy toxins irritate the body and nervous system creating an intense physical craving for more dairy foods and a psychological addiction for more dairy foods to stop these withdrawal symptoms. The dairy addict needs another dairy fix.

These physical and psychological withdrawal symptoms make it very difficult for a person to give up dairy or another favorite poison and this explains why so many have failed to give up unhealthful foods which they know are killing them slowly but surely.

Unfortunately, cutting back on dairy and other unhealthful allergens does not work either. The offending allergy food must be slowly decreased and then totally eliminated from the diet because the cells will continue to accumulate even small amounts of the dairy food, etc. and will never completely clean themselves until all types and all amounts of the allergens are removed from the diet permanently.

Various allergy-addiction health problems therefore cannot be effectively treated without identifying and eliminating the offending food or habit. Treatment for allergy will also fail unless systemic toxicity is treated with a complete program of detoxification and improvement in diet.

In addition to toxicity from unhealthful foods, other metabolic disorders, especially candidiasis, parasites and hypothyroidism contribute toward your body's inability to eliminate accumulating toxins. Waste products from millions of living candida organisms and parasites and their body parts, especially proteins, literally poison the intestines and the whole body making you even more toxic and overly sensitive or allergic and addicted to unhealthful foods, smoking, alcohol, street drugs and medical drugs.

Hypothyroidism is also a basic cause of allergy and other health problems in that deficient thyroid hormone disturbs the function of every cell in the body by decreasing your ability to metabolize food and eliminate toxins. Hypothyroidism, candidiasis, chronic Epstein-Barr virus, and parasites all cause inflammation, malabsorption syndrome, leaky gut syndrome, systemic toxicity, destruction of the immune system which in turn cause hypersensitivity allergy reactions. Therefore, these underlying conditions must be treated in any allergy treatment program. See the sections on hypothyroidism and candidiasis for more details.

Candidiasis, chronic Epstein-Barr virus, parasites and hypothyroidism are therefore causes of allergy and unless they are treated successfully and repeatedly once or twice a year, any treatment for allergy is likely to fail.

Test for food allergy with Dr. Steig Erlander's acid-alkaline pH urine test. Dr. Erlander discovered that food allergy is a special case of toxicity which creates an acid condition in the body. A special testing diet, called the alkaline potato diet, is allergy free for most people and is designed to alkalize and de-acidify the system. The idea is to alkalize the body with cooked vegetables and then systematically introduce a suspected allergenic food one at a time to see if the body has an acid or allergic reaction to that specific food.

The potato diet consists of cooked root and green leafy vegetables, potato or yams with each meal and also carrots, squash, beets, daikon, ginger, celery, greens, chives, parsley, salt, mild leafy herbs, water, herb tea and fresh carrot juice. Since allergy is caused mostly by proteins, all vitamins, grains and seed vegetables, broccoli, asparagus, tomatoes, peppers, eggplant, cauliflower, green beans, zucchini, onion, garlic, etc. are not eaten during the testing period. Make a large pot of soup from the above vegetables and eat it breakfast, lunch and dinner. In between meals, eat only apples, applesauce, apple juice, peaches, nectarines, pears, plums, prunes and fresh apricots or drink carrot juice plain or with celery, beet, parsley, etc. No condiments or other foods not listed are allowed during testing. Ask your doctor if you can stop all medication during this period.

Test the urine pH with Nitrazine testing paper which can be purchased without a prescription from a pharmacy. Tear off a 1½ inch strip of testing paper, sit on the toilet (guys, too), hold one end of the testing paper and urinate on the other end. The urine will change the color of the testing paper and you can compare the color to the color chart. A pH approaching 7.5 or blue indicates an alkaline or allergy free condition and a pH approaching 4.5 or yellow indicates an acid or allergy reaction. For infants, place a strip of testing paper in the diaper with a small piece of cellophane between the testing paper and the skin to avoid contamination of the testing paper. The baby's urine, however, will find its way to the testing paper.

Test your urine before you start the allergy testing program to see what reaction you are having to your present diet. Eat the potato diet three or more times a day and do not skip meals which causes an acid condition. Test your urine before each meal and 30, 60 and 90 minutes after each meal. After one or two days if the urine does not test blue or alkaline, test the individual foods in the potato diet itself until you identify and exclude the allergenic food. Many people have an allergy to potatoes and other nightshades, tomato, peppers and eggplant.

Make a list of suspected allergy foods beginning with the foods you eat the most. Eat the alkaline vegetables for breakfast but do not test a suspected allergen food at breakfast because the urine is usually lower in pH or acid and will confuse the testing results. Before lunch or dinner, test your urine pH. Along with your alkaline lunch or dinner, at the same meal, eat a good portion of the test food, wheat, for example, and retest the urine pH 30, 60 and 90 minutes after eating the potato diet and the test food. If you are allergic to the test food, your urine will test acid or yellow on the testing paper. Test only one suspected allergen food on any one particular day even if the test was negative at lunch. Continue eating the potato diet and test another food the next day, either at lunch or dinner.

When identified, eliminate all allergenic foods and find substitutes for them. Some alternative doctors recommend the rotation diet of eating tolerated foods not more often than every 5 days. It is said that allergenic foods can be added to the rotation diet later. I agree with eating tolerated non-allergy foods on a rotation basis because all of us tend to eat the same foods over and over to excess. However, I disagree with adding non-tolerated allergy foods on the rotation diet. Just because an allergy food does not appear to cause visible toxicity and symptoms does not mean that it does not cause underlying toxicity and health problems subclinically beyond our senses.

Treatment for allergy includes testing and therapy for hypothyroidism, candidiasis and parasites, a good cleansing and detoxification program, the cleansing diet, a series of colonics, herbal laxatives and the following supplements during active allergy symptoms and also periodically to prevent symptoms.

Build up the immune system with Selenium 100 mcg, zinc 15 mg, B-complex 25 mg, vitamin A 15,000 IU, and freeze-dried neonatal thyroid gland extract 2 to 10 tablets — all twice a day with lunch and dinner. Minimize systemic inflammatory and histamine reactions with quercetin 400 mg and bromelain 125 mg both taken 20 minutes before meals or, if you forget, during meals. 10 Standard Process (call 800-292-6699) Antronex tablets and vitamin C 1500 mg both 3 times a day with meals and freshly ground flax seed once a day in between meals will also help prevent and control systemic inflammatory and histamine reactions.

Chiropractic adjustments also stimulate and strengthen the immune system and can help turn arround an allergy attack.

ALMOND MILK

1½ cups raw almonds
2 tsp. or more vanilla extract
3 tbsp. or more raw honey, rice or barley syrup,
    or pure maple syrup (no formaldehyde)
½ tsp. or more sea salt

Soak the almonds overnight; afterward, discard the water. Blend the almonds with 1½ cups filtered water at high speed. During blending, add the vanilla, sweetener and salt. Blend until smooth periodically adding ice cubes to avoid destroying the living enzymes and nutrients with heat. Pour the contents into a 2 qt. container and add about a quart of water. Stir and taste test adding more vanilla, sweetener or salt as needed. If more sweetener is needed, pour a little milk into the blender and start the blender and then add the extra sweetener to mix it in easily. No need to strain but for special occasions when you are trying to impress a person who is not a health nut, strain the milk with a straining cloth or fine mesh stainless steel strainer. Store with a lid in the refrigerator. Serve alone or with cold or hot cereal, crumbled cornbread or cook with it instead of milk. It will keep for about 3 days and to keep it longer, pour the almond milk into used 16 oz. carrot juice bottles about three-quarters full and freeze them until needed. To thaw, boil some water, turn off the heat, place the frozen bottle of almond milk in the hot water until it partially melts, pour it into the blender (you can cut the plastic bottle to get the partially frozen milk out), blend, taste test and add a little vanilla, sweetener or salt to touch it up if necessary. Even unhealthy nuts, young and old, love almond milk!

Alternatives: You can also make milk out of cashews, pecans, walnuts, sunflower seeds, pumpkin seeds, brown rice, etc. either alone or in combination.

BEANS AND LENTILS

Clean beans or lentils by placing them on the kitchen counter to eliminate any bad ones, dirt or stones which could break your teeth or otherwise take the magic out of the meal. Slide a small group of them to one side; look them over and remove any debris; then slide them over as a group away from the others; continue this until they have been cleaned. Rinse in a colander and soak them for 8 to 16 hours to leach out enzyme-inhibitors which prevent proper digestion. Discard the soaking water. Cook beans or lentils with lots of water in a pyrex pot by bringing them to a boil and simmering until done. Beans usually take a couple hours and lentils less. Using a stainless steel spatula, stir more in the beginning, occasionally in the middle and more again in the end of cooking. Keep adding more water to make an ample amount of broth. When done, add any seasoning or other ingredients for that fresh taste. To thicken broth, if necessary, blend some of the beans or lentils and broth in a blender until smooth and add it back to the pot and continue simmering for another 10 minutes or the longer the better. Stir more often in this stage. If the broth becomes too thick, add a little water. Taste test and add more salt or seasoning. Serve over crumbled skillet bread or brown rice or on the side plain or topped with chopped leek, relish, cayenne hot pepper and cashew spread. In general, eat a moderate amount of beans and lentils at a time and not two days in a row to prevent indigestion. Lentils are easier to digest than beans, especially when sprouted first. Sometimes make double the amount, eat half and freeze the other half. Several different recipe ideas follow.

PINTO BEANS: 1 cup pinto beans; ½ tsp. cayenne pepper; ½ tsp. sea salt; garlic to taste. Always taste test and add more seasoning if necessary. Make lots of good broth and don't add other ingredients to avoid covering up the great flavor of pinto beans and be sure to serve them over crumbled cornbread or other skillet bread and top them off with cayenne hot sauce, chopped leeks and cashew spread almost Southern style meaning most Southerners back home never heard of cashew spread and they use lots of smelly onion instead of leek. *Alternative:* when cooked, add tomato sauce, honey, molasses, cumin, herb seasoning and lemon or lime juice and simmer briefly. Lentils are good this way also.

BABY LIMA BEANS: 1 cup baby lima beans or butter beans; ¼ tsp. cayenne pepper; ½ tsp. sea salt; garlic, herb seasoning and liquid aminos to taste. Stir often near the end because the broth gets thick. Serve with peeled ready-cut cooked tomato or fresh cut tomato on the side. Delicious.

GARBANZO BEANS: 1 cup garbanzo beans also known as chickpeas; ¼ tsp. cayenne pepper; ½ tsp. sea salt; garlic, cumin seed, herb seasoning and lemon or lime juice to taste. Cook the garbanzo beans until done, blend with a little of the cooking water until smooth. When blended, add chopped celery, carrots and parsley. Taste test and add more seasoning, especially cumin if needed. Serve over brown rice, millet or noodles.

GARBANZO BEAN DIP OR SANDWICH SPREAD: 1 cup garbanzo beans; ½ tsp. garlic powder; ½ cup minced parsley; 2 lemons juiced; 1 tbsp. ground cumin; 1 tbsp. liquid aminos; ½ tsp. sea salt; 1 cup cashew spread; 1 cup hulled sesame seeds. Toast half of the sesame seeds, cool, add to untoasted seeds and grind into a powder. Mix all of the ingredients together. Taste test. Chill and serve as a dip with sticks of carrots, celery, sunchokes, cauliflower, green pepper or blanched broccoli. Can also be served as a sandwich spread or thinned with water for a dressing or sauce.

LENTILS: 1 cup lentils; ¼ tsp. cayenne pepper; ½ tsp. sea salt; garlic, herb seasoning and liquid aminos to taste. When done, add chopped green pepper, carrot, celery and parsley. Note that lentils are very easy to sprout and these raw sprouts are much better for you than cooked lentils or beans. Add the sprouted lentils to salads, sandwiches, pates or cooked grains and vegetables in their raw state or briefly saute them in liquid aminos or water. Again, lentils are very easy to sprout and can be eaten raw, sauteed or cooked and should be eaten very often.

BEAN SAUCE: Beans or lentils made into a sauce seem lighter and easier to flavor and digest. Cook as above with the same seasoning. When done, blend beans and broth and probably a little extra water until smooth. Add chopped green pepper, carrot, celery and parsley and a little extra liquid aminos. Taste test adding more seasoning to taste. Briefly warm to serving temperature.

BREAD — SKILLET BREAD

Flour choices: cornmeal; equal parts cornmeal and corn flour; equal parts cornmeal and brown rice flour; equal parts spelt flour and brown rice flour; 1 part quinoa flour and 2 parts brown rice flour; 1 part buckwheat flour and 2 parts brown rice flour; 1 part millet flour and 2 parts brown rice flour; Mix a large bag of your favorite flour combination, label and store in freezer.

Many flour combinations are offered to encourage you to rotate your breads and grains and all foods by eating one type only once every five days. Most food allergy is caused by eating the same foods day after day, such as wheat bread, which is a common allergy food. With this in mind, the popular seven and ten grain breads, if eaten too often, can cause allergy. Stick to single or two grain bread to give you more control in rotating foods.

It is recommended that you grind only enough grain into flour for immediate use each day. Store excess flour and grains in the freezer and refrigerate all seeds and nuts. Ask your health food store manager to install a flour mill and display fresh grains in one or two pound plastic bags in the freezer section.

It is best to dextrinize grain, flour or meal (see Grains) to break down long chain carbohydrates into simpler starches for more effective digestion. Place flour or meal in an enameled iron skillet or baking pan and toast in a 425°F oven for 10 minutes; stir with a flat spatula and toast another 10 minutes; stir and reduce the heat to 350°F and toast for another 10 minutes or until a golden brown but not scorched or burned. Do not dextrinize seeds and seed meal.

RECIPE FOR SKILLET BREAD —

> 2 cups flour or flour/meal from above choices
> ½ cup toasted sesame seeds, partially ground
> ½ cup applesauce or cooked sweet potato, yam,
>   squash, pumpkin or carrot
> 3 pats melted butter
> 1 tbsp. onion powder
> 1 tsp. sea salt
> 2 tsp. baking powder
> 2 eggs, optional

Optional: add whole caraway seeds, dill weed, amaranth seed flour, a little honey, more onion powder, dry or chopped fresh herbs, garlic, etc.

Preheat the oven to 425°F. Butter an enameled iron skillet or Vision glass skillet and cover the bottom with extra toasted sesame seeds. Mix all ingredients together and add just enough water to keep the batter as thick as possible. Sprinkle extra sesame seeds or onion powder on top if you like. Bake at 425°F for 30 minutes. Remove from oven, use a knife around the perimeter to separate the bread from the sides of the skillet and use a spatula to separate the bread from the bottom. Spread out a clean dish cloth on the kitchen counter, cover the top of the bread with another dish towel or paper towel and turn the skillet over to put the bread on the counter. Cut and serve plain or with butter or cashew spread. Cut each slice crossways and use as a bottom for jelly or open face sandwiches. If a particular skillet bread recipe is too dry, add more applesauce, cooked vegetables or melted butter the next time and make notes.

BREAD — UNLEAVENED GRIDDLE PANCAKE BREAD

Unleavened bread tastes better and it is more digestible and wholesome. All baking powder and baking soda partially damage the flour. Yeast does not damage flour but avoid it because yeast can contribute toward candidiasis yeast infection.

Same choice of flour as the skillet bread recipe and it is recommended that you use dextrinized flour. Corn flour is better than cornmeal in this pancake recipe.

> 2 cups flour
> 1 cup toasted sesame seeds, partially ground
> 1 cup freshly ground sunflower, pumpkin or
>   flax seed
> 2 tbsp. or more onion powder
> 2 tsp. whole caraway seeds
> ½ tsp. sea salt

Optional: dill weed, dry or chopped fresh herbs, garlic, cooked quinoa, etc. Preheat the griddle to 400°F and we use a large non stick surface griddle. Mix all ingredients together and add just enough water to make it thin enough to spread with a spoon on the griddle into 3 or 4 inch pancakes. Brown and turn over several times until golden brown. Leftover pancakes can be reheated in the toaster or oven. Serve as bread with meals, as snacks, bottoms for jelly or openface sandwiches, fold over as taco shells, toast as chips, etc. Toasted sesame seeds give bread, grains and vegetables a great taste. Place 2 to 4 lb. hulled sesame seeds in a large baking pan. Toast in a 400°F oven, set the timer for 15 min., turn with a flat spatula, continue until golden brown, cool, grind half, mix together, store in refrigerator and enjoy.

BREAD — SKILLET BREAD DRESSING

6 - 8 cups cubed skillet bread
6 stalks chopped celery — sauteed
2 - 3 chopped green peppers — sauteed
2 - 4 cloves pressed garlic — sauteed
½ cup minced fresh parsley
1 cup sliced mushrooms
2 tbsp. onion powder or granules
2 tsp. each rosemary, sage and thyme
2 cloves pressed garlic
1 tsp. sea salt

Bake at least 2 batches of skillet bread, cool and cube into bite size pieces. Saute the celery, green pepper and garlic in a hot iron skillet with liquid aminos. Mix all of the ingredients in a large bowl, moisten with a little liquid aminos and/or a little water but not much because when it marinates, it gets more moist and, of course, more tasty. Taste test and add more seasoning according to your own taste. Cover or place in plastic bags and marinate 8 hours or longer. To serve, heat up briefly to take the chill off and serve with walnut gravy or it can also be used as a stuffing.

Delicious. This recipe makes a lot of dressing because everyone loves it and you can serve leftovers the next day. Share it with friends or reduce each ingredient to make less dressing. Dressing lovers may wonder where the chopped sauteed onions are. Onions cause indigestion, gas and bad breath.

CANDIDIASIS CAUSES MANY ILLNESSES AND DISEASES

Chronic candidiasis or yeast syndrome is a very common and very serious underlying metabolic disorder which can totally destroy your health, body, mind and spirit, and it is often overlooked, misdiagnosed and ridiculed. Failure to properly diagnose and treat candidiasis and other underlying metabolic disorders invites cancer, arthritis, emotional and mental problems and other illnesses. Candidiasis is often a cause of chronic Epstein-Barr virus.

Candida albicans, a yeast-like germ, can be cultured in healthy individuals from the intestines, anus, nose, throat and vagina. Its harmless numbers are kept under control by the more numerous friendly acidolphilus germs. The problems begin when the candida organisms overpopulate and outnumber the friendly germs, its enemy. This overpopulation and subsequent damage to the body is called candidiasis. Candidiasis can cause severe systemic toxicity, severe inflammatory conditions and severe immune deficiency making its victim more susceptible to other illnesses. Candida cell wall components, antigens and other toxins from millions of candida organisms can cause significant destruction by free radical damage and by generation of acetaldehyde, a toxin which can cause many central nervous system symptoms. Some candida organisms can reduce acetaldehyde to ethanol alcohol to produce a state of chronic alcohol intoxication.

Candida can invade mucosal and cutaneous tissue causing thrush and onychomycosis; it can invade the esophagus, lungs, urinary tract, eye, liver, heart, central nervous system and occasionally, the bloodstream causing more serious illnesses. It can cause symptoms in every system of the body, with the gastrointestinal, genitourinary, nervous, endocrine, immune and nervous systems being the most affected. Vaginal yeast infections are often caused by candida.

Candida overgrowth weakens the immune system by these yeast germs penetrating and damaging the intestinal mucosa allowing increased abnormal absorption of poison and suppress the immune factors in the mucosal wall. The immune complexes formed by the yeast are also immunosuppressive. When the immune system is damaged, candida will overgrow rapidly.

Risk factors and causes of candida overgrowth include most frequently, overuse of wide-spectrum antibiotics which kills the unfriendly and friendly germs but does not kill the resistant yeast germ, candida, therefore causing it to overpopulate. The friendly germs are the natural enemy of candida germs and normally keep them under control.

Dr. Robert Mendelsohn, M.D. states that the vast majority of antibiotics prescribed by doctors are unnecessary, inappropriate and ineffective. If antibiotic therapy is needed to treat some serious health problem, anti-fungal candida medication, i.e., Nystatin or some natural alternative, such as hydrogen peroxide, should be prescribed as recommended by alternative medical doctors to kill the candida germs thereby preventing candidiasis as a result of taking antibiotics.

Otherwise, untreated candidiasis causes frequent infections creating a greater likelihood for the use or overuse of antibiotics, which causes more severe candidiasis and more infections and more antibiotics in an increasing vicious cycle of illness and disease.

If you do not want to take Nystatin, which can cause some liver toxicity, note that lots of garlic has been shown to be more effective than Nystatin in controlling candida and also see treatment below.

Corticosteroids, immunosuppressants, oral contraceptives and such anti-ulcer drugs as Tagamet and Zantac promote the overgrowth of candida.

Sugar, white flour, pasteries, all dairy foods, too much fruit,

too many sweets including honey, alcohol, processed carbohydrates, nutrient deficiencies of vitamin A, viatmin B6, zinc,
selenium, magnesium, essential fatty acids, folic acid and iron from
eating processed foods, insufficient hydrochloric acid and pancreatic digestive enzymes, impaired liver function, diabetes
mellitus, thyroid diseases, other underlying diseases and stress can
cause candidiasis, according to Dr. William Crook, M.D. in *The
Yeast Connection*.

Much like hypothyroidism, allergy, systemic toxicity, free
radical pathology and chronic Epstein-Barr virus, candidiasis symptoms include toxicity, low immune system, increased susceptibility
to infection and degenerative diseases, such as, arthritis,
cardiovascular disease, cancer, AIDS, etc., chronic fatigue,
decreased interest in sex, bloating, gas, intestinal cramps, rectal
itching, diarrhea, constipation, frequent bladder infections, earache,
menstrual complaints, vaginal yeast infections, brain fog, depression, irritability, mood swings, poor concentration, nervous
breakdown, psoriasis, drowsiness, insomnia, headaches, sensation of head swelling, weak, shaky muscles, sore throat, crying
spells, chest congestion, cold extremities, chills, low fever,
hypersensitivity toward light and sound, and many other common
illnesses. Note that stubborn nail fungus is often caused by
candidiasis.

Candidiasis infection is also common in chronic Epstein-Barr
virus and AIDS patients. Prolonged oral thrush with progression
to candida esophagitis is found frequently and is thought to be a
forerunner of AIDS. This is quite understandable in that candidiasis
damages and destroys the immune system and AIDS is, of course,
an immune deficiency disease.

People with chronic Epstein-Barr virus usually also have candidiasis and their symptoms are similar. However, the following
comparison of symptoms may help you distinguish between the
two conditions. Chronic Epstein-Barr virus symptoms include:
intermittant attacks; no craving for sugar and carbohydrates; very
little gastrointestinal upset; no food allergies; no skin rashes or
nail infections; no postnasal drip; no hormonal influence; and no
muscle fatigue upon exertion; whereas, candidiasis symptoms
include: progressive, worsening course; irresistible craving for
sugar and carbohydrates; extreme constipation, gas, bloating,
distension; extreme food sensitivies, which get worse; butterfly

rash on face, athlete's foot, nail infections; postnasal drip almost constantly; premenstrual and menstrual complaints; and muscle and joint pains most of the time.

The standard test used for candidiasis is a stool analysis which is often negative when candidiasis is present but your orthodox doctor may report the negative lab report as definitive proof that you do not have candidiasis when you may have it. The problem is that the stool analysis is not a specific test for candidiasis and its findings are inconclusive and misleading.

The rectal swab test for candida in the mucus and feces in the entrance of the rectum is accurate. The test requires a good amount of effort and is not often done partly due to the work involved and also most orthodox doctors simply are not very interested in candidiasis or any other underlying metabolic disorder despite its great importance in causing most illnesses and diseases. Make as many telephone calls to alternative doctors as necessary to find someone who will do the rectal swab test or refer you to a lab who will take the specimen.

Consult a nutritionally oriented medical doctor who is either a holistic doctor, clinical ecologist or a doctor who does chelation therapy or see a nutritional chiropractor or naturopath. In addition to the more accurate rectal swab test and any other lab tests, your alternative doctor will consider your detailed medical history, specifically including: factors, such as a history of taking antibiotics, which might predispose to overgrowth of candida; history of previous candida infections; a possible correlation between increasing candida antigen levels and increasing systemic symptoms; history of food, mold or chemical sensitivity; presence of medical conditions associated with candidiasis; and a positive score on a candidiasis questionnaire (available by request from Dr. Deal).

According to Dr. Luc De Schepper, M.D., the most accurate test for candidiasis is the CandiSpere Enzyme Immuno Assay Test (CEIA) from a small blood sample. Available from CERODEX Lab, P.O. Box 1151, Oklahoma City, OK 73070, telephone (405) 288-2383 but call Meditrend who does the marketing for them and their address is P.O. Box 14493, Albuquerque, NM 87191-4493, telephone (800) 545-8900 or (505) 292-0700.

Successful treatment of candidiasis involves reducing predisposing factors to candida overgrowth, improving immune function and inhibiting overpopulation. Curtail predisposing factors by: having your doctor consider getting you off antibiotics, Tagamet, Zantac, corticosteroids, immune-suppressing drugs and any drug which promotes the overgrowth of candida; following the candida control diet by avoiding refined sugars, corn syrup, fruit juices, honey, maple syrup, yeast or mold foods, alcohol, cheese and all dairy, dried fruits, melons, peanuts, known or suspected allergic foods; limit high carbohydrate vegetables, potato, corn, yam and parsnips; improve digestion with plant enzymes, pancreatic enzymes, hydrochloric acid and carrot acidolphilus and control overeating; and improve impaired liver function by a series of colonics to reduce intestinal absorption of toxic bowel compounds and bacteria, fungus and food antigens all of which the liver would otherwise be required to detoxify; also improve liver problems by following the therapies outlined under the section on liver.

Improve immune function to control candida overgrowth by: eliminating, if possible, under the supervision of your alternative medical doctor, the drugs which damage or destroy the immune system; avoid chemotherapy, radiation, x-rays, environmental chemicals and pollutants, nutritional deficiencies, alcohol, cigarettes, coffee and stress; seek alternative treatment for hypothroidism, low hydrochloric stomach acid output, cancer, diabetes and other diseases which cause or aggravate candidiasis; eat Dr. Deal's Delicious Detox Diet; take the supplements recommended below including thymus gland which is known to improve immunity.

Inhibit candida overgrowth by reducing the predisposing factors, by strengthening the immune system and by taking 2 to 4 oz. Dr. Donsbach's Super Oxy Tonic (premixed hydrogen peroxide in a base of aloe juice) before bed and upon rising on an empty stomach. Also take daily delayed released caprylic acid 1 gram, grapefruit seed extract 250 mg or 3 drops in citrus juice twice a day, milk lactose free acidolphilus 2 capsules, and liberal amounts of ginger and garlic (found to be more effective than Nystatin) all with meals; calcium-magnesium butyrate 1200 mg with meals will help heal the intestinal lining inflamed and made porous by candidiasis; drink 8 oz. water with 10 drops Aerox or Aerobic 7 (stabilized oxygen) three times a day on an empty stomach; drink 1 to 2 quarts of pau d'arco or taheebo tea daily; upon rising, grind

2 oz. of fresh, whole flax seed and blend with 1½ cups pure water, 2 ice cubes, and the juice of one freshly squeezed lemon; and drink sarsapirilla tea mid morning, mid afternoon and before bed to absorb colon and candida toxins; also consider taking freeze-dried neonatal thymus gland 2 tablets with meals especially for weakened immune systems and history of frequent infections.

All of the above remedies are presented because chronic candidiasis is a very stubborn and difficult infection to treat effectively and some persons may have to do everything possible to get it under control. However, most people respond well by taking only the most important supplements, which are hydrogen peroxide, grapefruit seed extract, caprylic acid, acidolphilus, pau d'arco tea and Aerox or Aerobic 7.

Note that Dr. Donsbach's Super Oxy Tonic hydrogen peroxide is available from Professional Products, 424 Calle Primera, San Ysidro, CA 92173, telephone (800) 767-8585 or (619) 428-7667. In that hydrogen peroxide itself may cause some free radicals, always take along with it several catalase and superoxide dismutase tablets to neutralize any free radicals.

If candidiasis tends to recur, have your alternative doctor test you for low hydrochloric stomach acid output which could be a cause of candidiasis or other infection. In addition to digesting food, hydrochloric acid in the tissues and blood also kills candida and other germs to keep them under control as one of your body's normal defense mechanisms. It is also worth noting that low hydrochloric acid can be a cause of hypothyroidism or hyperthyroidism.

Take a series of colonics, one a day for 7 days, then one a week and repeat the 7 day colonic program every 6 weeks to clean out the vast amount of toxins deposited in the intestines by millions of candida organisms.

Treat candidiasis for a minimum of 3 to 8 weeks and longer in some severe cases. Most importantly, you must repeat the treatment every 6 months or even every 4 months because, unfortunately, candidiasis tends to recur over and over unless all the damage, predisposing factors and immune dysfunction have been corrected and in some persons, this may be almost impossible.

Vaginal candida yeast infection can be effectively treated with the above protocol. Also, potassium sorbate cream vaginal suppositories and douching with pau d'arco tea are helpful.

Are you feeling encouraged or discouraged? Can you gather the will and strength to treat candidiasis effectively? Try it because you will start to feel better. You may get temporarily worse as a result of the die-off response from killing the organisms so effectively with this treatment but you will be feeling better soon. Once you get it under control, you can start to enjoy life more fully.

CARPAL TUNNEL SYNDROME TREATMENT

It is heartbreaking to witness the slow disability and death of a person's arms, wrists and hands, when in most cases, it is totally unnecessary. Orthodox treatment usually consists of drugs, wrist braces and surgery often with a poor outcome leaving the patient crippled physically and emotionally.

It may come as a surprise to the medical Establishment that a person's arms, wrists and hands have a nerve and blood supply from the cervical plexus and if this supply is interfered with, the upper extremities wither and die as in carpal tunnel syndrome. Therefore, normalizing the nerve and blood supply to the upper extremities is very important to bring life back to your arms, wrists and hands.

Sleeping on the abdomen is perhaps the number one cause of carpal tunnel syndrome and ALSO MOST NECK AND SHOULDER PROBLEMS. You would be disappointed to learn that not one of my carpal tunnel patients has been told this by his orthodox doctor. When you sleep on your stomach with your head turned to one side or the other or when you have your arms and hands higher than your shoulders, the neck and shoulder muscles and spine are twisted causing interference to the nerves and blood supply to the arms, wrists, hands, shoulders and neck. Restore life to them by sleeping on your back or your side with your arms and hands below your shoulders. Ask your spouse or family to remind you or even awaken you to help you stop sleeping on your abdomen.

Chiropractic adjustments and massage of the cervical and thoracic spine and the elbow, wrist and hands are vitally important to normalize nerve and blood supply to take care of the carpal tunnel problem and most neck and shoulder muscle and spinal problems.

Massage the neck, shoulder, arms, wrist and hands several times a day if possible. Ask your spouse, family and friends to help massage you and you can do most of it yourself, at home and at work during breaks. Why not massage your arm and hand while you talk on the telephone, etc.? Lengthen and relax the muscles between the shoulder and elbow and between the elbow and hand by massaging toward the joint to relax the muscle tendon periosteal connective tissue attachments. Put some massage lotion on the skin, find a sore or tight spot and massage it toward the closest joint. It is best to first apply a moist heat pad for 15 minutes before and after the massage. If heat causes too much swelling, try ice packs instead or use both. Massage flax seed oil into the skin of the arms, wrists and hands. Use a moist heating pad for 15 minutes beforehand. Massage all the painful and tight places with flax seed oil. Afterward, on the worst spots, apply lots of flax seed oil to the skin, wrap a thin wash cloth around the area, saturate it with flax seed oil, wrap a piece of plastic around the area, wrap a heating pad around the plastic and apply heat for 15 minutes. Move the treatment to other bad areas and repeat the procedure. Apply heat for only 15 minutes in any one location. Always set a timer and never go to sleep with the heating pad on because heating an area for longer than 20 minutes or so will cause muscle cramping and edema. Sears has a cuff-type heating pad but it is not the moist heat type.

In addition to chiropractic and massage, the nerve and blood supply to the upper extremities can be normalized by eliminating lung, liver and gall bladder inflammation and toxicity, which is referred back to the mid-thoracic spine (the nerve supply to the lungs, liver and gall bladder) causing inflammation, swelling, muscle tightness, spinal fixation and interference with the nerve and blood supply to the arms, wrists and hands. The lungs, liver and gall bladder, as well as the rest of the body, can be detoxified by the Detox Diet, eliminating the dairy and sugar which poison the lungs and eliminating the free oils, fats, fried foods, alcohol, coffee, overeating, etc. which poison the liver and gall bladder.

Take vitamin B6 50 to 200 mg daily. Freshly grind 2 tablespoons whole flax seed (not flax meal) in a small coffee grinder, place in a blender with 8 oz. water, 3 ice cubes and the juice of a lemon, blend until smooth and drink upon rising or later in the day.

Continue the above treatment for 12 weeks or longer. In that about 95% of us have, somehow, given up on life and the will to live to the maximum, counsel the patient to encourage him to want to get well. Often, carpal tunnel syndrome patients sabotage an effective natural treatment program to avoid responsibility in work and relationships. Feeling sorry for yourself, making yourself dependent on everyone and taking drugs and getting surgery is easier than taking responsibility, improving your diet and following a complete treatment program.

CASHEW SPREAD

1 ½ cups raw cashews (soak overnight in refrigerator)
½ tsp. sea salt
~~¼ tsp. cayenne pepper~~
~~½ tsp. garlic powder or granules~~
½ cup filtered water
3 - 5 ice cubes

Grind the cashews and blend all ingredients in a Vita-Mix or blender until smooth, using a spatula to scrape down the sides. If necessary, add just enough water or another ice cube to keep the ingredients moving in the blender but don't add too much to keep it as thick as possible. If too thin, add more cashews but grind them first. Shake the blender to keep the ingredients moving and blend until smooth. Place in a covered container and store in the refrigerator to set up or it can be used right away.

Use as a mayonnaise, sour cream or cheese substitute, spread for vegetables, bread, crackers, chips, etc.

Use as a salad dressing by thinning it out with a little water and by adding more lemon or lime juice, various herbs, honey, sea salt, sliced stuffed green olives and toasted sesame seeds.

MACARONI AND CHEESE SUBSTITUTE: Enjoy cashew spread as a cheese substitute for macaroni and cheese by blending 8 oz. of pimentos along with the other ingredients. Try corn elbow macaroni. Cook the macaroni and drain well. Add cashew-pimento sauce, stir a little and serve. Alternative: Mix macaroni and sauce and place in a buttered skillet or baking dish and bake at 425°F for 20 - 30 minutes. If any leftovers, heat up the next day in a buttered skillet.

PESTO SAUCE: Try cashew spread as a pesto sauce by adding ¼ cup minced fresh parsley, 1 tsp. sweet basil (or more if fresh) and extra garlic to your own taste. Blend all ingredients together and serve with hot pasta. Pine nuts can be substituted for cashews.

ESSENTIAL OILS SPREAD OR SAUCE: In a coffee grinder or Vita-Mix, grind equal parts of any or all the following raw seeds high in essential linoleic and linolenic acids: flax, sesame, pumpkin, sunflower. Blend until smooth with sea salt, cayenne pepper, garlic, lemon or lime, water and ice cubes in the amounts listed in the cashew spread recipe. Cashews can be added to make the sauce more creamy. Serve as a spread or sauce for pasta, vegetables and grains or add water and more lemon juice to make a salad dressing.

CASSEROLE

1 lb. firm tofu
2 - 3 large eggplants
1 bag whole wheat pasta
28 oz. ready cut tomatoes
8 oz. tomato paste (cont. next page)

16 oz. Old El Paso Thick 'n' Chunky Salsa
6 sliced mushrooms
1 chopped green pepper
1 - 2 bunches spinach, chopped
15 oz. sliced ripe olives
½ cup chopped fresh fennel and/or
1 tsp. fennel powder
2 tsp. toasted sesame seeds
2 tsp. herb seasoning
½ tsp. thyme
½ tsp. garlic powder or granules
½ tsp. sea salt
¼ tsp. cayenne
1 lemon, juiced
8 oz. tomato sauce
3 eggs

Cut tofu into small pieces, sprinkle with herb mix, garlic, cayenne pepper and liquid aminos, mix and bake in a buttered skillet or pan at 550º F for 20 minutes, remove from oven, add liquid aminos and turn over with a spatula, continue baking until brown and chewy, checking every 10 minutes or so. Likewise, cut the eggplant into small pieces, sprinkle with the same ingredients and bake using the same method as the tofu except after the first 20 minutes, add a little water to keep it moist. When the tofu and eggplant are done, remove from the oven, add liquid aminos, stir with a spatula and empty both into a covered dish until you are ready for them. Turn the oven down to 350º F to get ready for the casserole. Chop and saute the green pepper, fennel and mushrooms in a little liquid aminos. Clean, chop and steam the spinach, drain, press well with paper towels to remove water and place in a large mixing bowl. Cook pasta, drain and place in the mixing bowl and right away add and mix all the spices, sesame seeds, lemon juice, chopped sauteed vegetables, sliced olives and the tofu and eggplant to keep the pasta from sticking together. Drain the cut tomatoes and salsa well, saving the liquid for other recipes and mix with the tomato paste in a small bowl and add to the other ingredients in the mixing bowl. Also add 3 eggs. Mix and taste test, adding more seasoning if necessary. Butter a large baking dish and spread the tomato sauce over the bottom and then sprinkle some toasted sesame seeds over it. Pour in the ingredients and press down firm. Bake at 350º F for 30 minutes and before the last 10 minutes put cashew spread on top and continue baking. Slice and serve. Can be made in the morning or the day before because it gets better when the spices have time to blend in. Freeze any leftovers for another great dinner. Can also be served with a tomato sauce on top.

CHILDREN

What the mother and father feed their baby will determine its immune system defense capabilities, its weight and its emotional, mental and physical health for the rest of its life. Failure to understand this may condemn your children to a life of allergy problems, frequent infections, obesity, hyperactivity, emotional instability, mental disease, health problems, cancer and other degenerative diseases and misery.

The child's diet and eating habits can be no better than the parents. This is the first obstacle in giving nutritional counseling for babies and children. First and foremost, the parents may avoid and discredit any healthful advice because it means they will have to give up their favorite poisons and bad habits themselves.

How can a doctor or nutritionist convince parents to eliminate dairy and sugar, for example in their child's diet when the parents are not willing to give up these unhealthful foods themselves?

How can the parents be educated about the dangers of immunization for their children when the parents are reluctant to buck a hostile army of Establishment doctors, school nurses, teachers, dietitians, government bureaucrats, media representatives, family members and in-laws who want the parents to poison their child with toxic vaccines just because everyone else is foolish enough to do it?

Your challenge as parents is to protect yourselves and your children from orthodox doctors and government health agencies who push processed foods, drugs and vaccines down your throat.

The following information on diet for infants and children will, for the sake of brevity, be given in summary form. You are encouraged to read *Everywoman's Book* by Paavo Airola, Ph.D., *The Encyclopedia of Baby and Child Care*, by Lendon Smith, M.D. (omit the dairy), *How to Raise a Healthy Child in Spite of Your Doctor*, by Robert Mendelsohn, M.D. and *Fit For Life II: Living Health*, by Harvey and Marilyn Diamond.

Breastfeeding: Dr. Mendelsohn recommends breastfeeding for the following reasons: Mother's milk is nature's perfect food for babies. Breast milk contains natural immune factors that inhibit the growth of bacteria and viruses and prevent many allergies. Breastfeeding establishes the miracle of bonding between the mother and her baby, providing a lifetime of emotional and psychological rewards. Breastfeeding helps prevent hemorrhage in the mother and also helps her return to her normal weight. Breastfeeding provides some measure of natural contraception protection by causing the reproductive cycle to move into a dormant stage. If the mother cannot breastfeed, a wet nurse should be substituted.

Bottlefeeding: Bottlefeeding may be more convenient but cow's milk and formulas make your baby sick despite claims to the contrary by orthodox doctors and dairy and formula salesmen. Cow's milk contains large fat globules and 300% more casein protein than mother's milk and other proteins which the baby cannot digest causing allergies, mucus, free radical pathology, constipation, colitis, colon cancer, other cancers, infections, especially involving the lungs, ears, eyes, throat and sinuses, kidney problems, associated fluid retention and weight gain, headache, migraine, iron-deficiency anemia, arteriosclerosis and many other illnesses.

Dr. Francis Pottenger in a famous study of 900 cats reported that cats fed on pasteurized milk and meat failed to thrive and developed heart disease, cancer, kidney and thyroid disease, pneumonia, paralysis, loss of teeth, arthritis, difficulty in labor, diminished sexual interest, diarrhea, irritability, liver impairment and osteoporosis. Is this what you want for your family?

Commercial formulas and commercial baby food made from dairy, soy, and overcooked vegetables and fruit are dead junk food containing too much or too little sodium, cheap palm oils, sugar, corn syrup, irritating synthetic vitamins and chemical additives.

But they are convenient for the mother. Note that processed baby foods contain little or no essential linolenic or linoleic fatty acids necessary for brain development and overall health. Where is the baby supposed to get the necessary food enzymes and essential oils for proper digestion, assimilation and elimination? From fresh, living foods not from processed dead foods in cans and jars.

Substitutes: Dr. Airola provides recipes for formulas made from raw goat's milk, vegetable broth and soy. As many as 15% of infants are allergic to cow or goat milk, pasteurized or raw. If your baby is not allergic, raw goat milk is better than pasteurized cow's milk. Soy and nuts are common allergens and if they are substituted for mother's milk, the infant should be tested for food allergy using Dr. Erlander's urine pH test at home or you may have your alternative doctor conduct other allergy tests.

Raw and fresh, cooked vegetables and fruit provide living enzymes and nutrients far superior to commercial baby food. These fresh foods can be prepared with common blenders, kitchen machines and strainers.

Diet: The newborn should be nursed for at least 18 months or longer. The Hunzas breastfeed for 2 to 3 years. Breastfed babies do not require solid food for the first year of life and should not be given solid food for at least 4 months. Bottlefed babies should not be given solid food for at least 4 months. The baby's digestive system is not yet well enough developed to process solid food, particularly protein. The enzyme to digest rice cereal, for example, is not adequate until 4 months of age. Solid foods, especially proteins, can cause lifelong allergy and illness and they can choke the baby because the swallowing mechanism is not fully developed. Raw goat's milk and soy milk, if tolerated, can be given to bottlefed babies only if the mother cannot produce milk or if a wet nurse cannot be found.

The baby should be observed closely to be sure there is no visible allergic or behavioral reaction, such as excessive crying or fussiness. Dr. Mendelsohn states that a child's nutritional requirements, including protein and calcium, can be met without cow or goat milk.

Rice or barley cereal can be added in small amounts at 7 to 10 months of age. Banana, pear, applesauce, carrot, squash and sweet potato can be added in small amounts at 9 to 12 months. Some eggs and fish can be added after the age of 1 year.

Organically fed and antibiotic, chemical free clean fish, beef, lamb, chicken and turkey can also be added if available. Limit new foods to one per month and watch for reactions, crying, irritability, rash, constipation, diarrhea, congestion, infections, etc. Individual appetites vary. Feeding on demand after 1 year of age is usually the best guide. Appetites tend to decrease between ages 2 and 4. Personally, with the exception of vitamin C, I would not give my baby synthetic vitamins or minerals derived from mineral rocks. Instead, I would give natural vitamins and minerals from herbs and plants and from organs and glands of organically fed newborn calves. If anemic, I would give iron ferritin from purified spleen ferritin in an isolated, individually resolved, high molecular weight compound, not a ferritin-complex.

Childhood Immunization: Dr. Mendelsohn "would urge you to reject all inoculations for your child" because "there is no convincing scientific evidence that mass inoculations can be credited with eliminating any childhood disease (including polio). There are significant risks associated with every immunization and numerous contraindications that may make it dangerous for the shots to be given to your child. While the myriad short-term hazards of most immunizations are known but rarely explained, no one knows the long-term consequences of injecting foreign proteins into the body of your child."

How to Raise a Healthy Child in Spite of Your Doctor by Dr. Mendelsohn outlines the reasons why you should not immunize your child with vaccines.

For more information, listen to the tapes "Vaccines and the Bible" and "Drugs and the Bible" by Pastor Sheldon Emry available for $10 each from Lord's Covenant Church, P.O. Box 157, Sandpoint, Idaho   83864, telephone (208) 265-5405. Read *Vaccination: The Silent Killer* by Ida Honorof and E. McBean and read *DPT: A Shot in the Dark* by Harris Coulter, M.D. and Barbara Fisher. Join the organization Dissatisfied Parents Together (DPT), 128 Branch Road, Vienna, Virginia   22180, telephone (703) 938-3783 and ask for a local member in your area.

Listen to these tapes, read these books and join alternative organizations to arm yourself against attack by bureaucrats and doctors and "well intentioned" in-laws who think it is best to "protect" your child with vaccines. Talk to parents who have vaccine damaged children or children killed by vaccines. Request literature from DPT to look at the photographs of normal, healthy, happy babies before they were damaged or killed by vaccines.

When a baby or child gets sick, the first question to ask is, ''When was he or she immunized?'' Most reactions to vaccines occur within two weeks after immunization and some show up years later in the form of learning disabilities, hyperactivity, cancer, multiple sclerosis, arthritis, heart disease and other degenerative diseases.

Write to the National Health Federation, P.O. Box 688, Monrovia, CA 91016, telephone (818) 357-2181 to request the immunization packet outlining how to use constitutional rights, religious affiliation or medical excuse to avoid immunization for school or travel.

Go to a nutritionally oriented medical doctor and ask for a letter stating that your child cannot be immunized for medical reasons. Ask the school and medical bureaucrats to sign a statement stating that immunization will absolutely not injure or kill your child and if so, that they take full personal and financial responsibility to pay for any medical treatment or claims against them. As a last resort, hire a Christian attorney to protect your child from the government medicrats. Mandatory immunization is another good reason to keep your child out of atheistic government public schools and to send them to private Christian schools or to teach them at home.

CHRONIC EPSTEIN-BARR VIRUS

Epstein-Barr virus is a type of herpes virus easily passed along in the saliva. The virus infects the B Lymphocytes of the white blood cells in the bone marrow that normally manufacture antibodies against disease. After the acute phase of infection, a few latent Epstein-Barr viruses remain in some of the B-cells only to flare up again during stress when the immune system is weak, especially when chronically weakened by chronic candidiasis. The person usually gets candidiasis first which wears down the immune system making him susceptible to Epstein-Barr virus.

Chronic Epstein-Barr virus can be classified as an underlying metabolic disorder and one of those important conditions commonly overlooked, misdiagnosed or minimized by orthodox doctors. The virus wears down the immune system causing a variety of illnesses and diseases unnecessarily, in that they could have been prevented if Epstein-Barr virus had been treated effectively with natural therapies to build up the immune system.

As a result of the acute and latent phases, the diagnostic picture for chronic Epstein-Barr virus is complicated and like hypoglycemia, the patient's medical history of related clinical symptoms is the most important factor in its diagnosis. Laboratory tests for chronic Epstein-Barr virus may show EBV-VCA-IgG antibody 1:640 or higher, low or absent anti-VCA-IgM, EAD detectable, EAR detectable, EBNA relatively low compared with the IgG, for instance 40, T4/T8 Ratio reduced in ratio and a significant reduction in suppressor cells in the acute phase.

Most importantly, make the diagnosis from the symptoms of chronic Epstein-Barr virus, which include a variety of non-specific conditions ranging from exhaustion, muscle pain or weakness, unusual muscle fatigue, relapsing, intermittent symptoms, a history of illness lasting more than three months, brain fog, mononucleosis kissing disease, recurrent sore throat, colds and painful lymph nodes in the neck, depression, severe mood swings. Candidiasis is usually found also in every case of chronic Epstein-Barr virus and is thought to be a causative factor.

Treatment consists of lots of rest and a complete detoxification and healing program. Linus Pauling recommends oral or intravenous vitamin C 30 g if tolerated or cut back the dosage if necessary. Start with 2 g several times a day and build up the dosage and when discontinuing vitamin C, always slowly reduce the dosage over a period of weeks to prevent rebound scurvy symptoms. In his book *Peak Immunity*, Dr. Luc De Schepper, M.D. (2901 Wilshire Blvd., Suite 435, Santa Monica, CA 90403, telephone (213) 828-4480) recommends two injections per week for several weeks of desiccated liver, folic acid, AMP and vitamin B5. Dr. De Schepper also recommends an immune-stimulating diet high in fiber from grains, vegetables and fruit; beta carotene containing vegetables, such as carrots, spinach, sweet potatoes, parsley, kale and collards, perhaps supplemented with 25,000 units of beta carotene tablets twice a day; vitamin E foods, such as eggs and spinach supplemented with 400 IU vitamin E daily; vitamin C foods, such as citrus, berries, tomatoes, potatoes, cauliflower and corn; zinc foods, such as pumpkin seeds and eggs and supplemented with 50 mg orotate zinc. He also prescribes Co-enzyme Q10 60 to 100 mg daily, germanium 250 to 500 mg daily and highly recommended are Polyzym 22 or Wobemugos up to 10 tablets three times daily (General Research Lab., 8900 Winnetka Ave., Northridge, CA 91324, telephone (818) 349-9911), hydrogen peroxide (use Dr. Donsbach's Super Oxy Plus Aloe Tonic with hydrogen peroxide 2 to 4 oz. before bed and upon arising), Aerox (Aerobic 7 is equivalent to Aerox, contact Aerobic Life Products, P.O. Box 28802, Dallas, TX 75228, telephone (214) 327-0707 — drink 8 oz. water with 10 drops Aerobic 7 three times a day), homeopathic herbs Rheum. Palmatum, Forsythia suspensa and Isatis tintoria and acupuncture. Exercise daily to eliminate toxins and it is best to exercise first thing in the morning when you have more energy.

Contact the support group, National CEBV Syndrome Association, P.O. Box 230108, Portland, OR 97223, telephone (503) 684-5261.

DAIRY DISASTER

Passed off as natural and healthful, DAIRY is actually one of the worst foods you can eat, causing many allergy and health problems. Since it is a favorite food, it is also one of the hardest to give up because everyone loves his milk, yogurt, cheese and ice cream.

When given the recommendation to eliminate all DAIRY from your diet, would most of you rather ignore the dangers of eating it; would you continue eating it; would you pretend that your health problems are not caused by eating dairy; would you get rid of the doctor trying to take away one of your favorite poisons; and would you run to an Establishment doctor or orthodox nutritionist who would let you get away with poisoning yourself with dairy foods by telling you the fairy tale fib that milk is nature's perfect food and that any doctor who says differently is a quack?

No one likes to give up dairy because it tastes good and gives you energy. You don't like to be told what to eat and what not to eat. And you, like all of us, may not like to face up to unpleasant realities.

Advising you that eating dairy is self-destructive will often cause a negative response and defensive behavior. You may not like having your toes stepped on even when you have asked for advice.

Having said that you may not like to hear the good advice that eliminating dairy will improve your health, please allow me to present the evidence against dairy foods.

"But how will I get adequate calcium if I give up dairy?" is usually the first excuse made by dairy lovers. The dairy lobby has done a good job convincing us that dairy foods are a good source of calcium to make strong bones and prevent osteoporosis but the dairy industry has been less than truthful in this regard.

Dairy foods do have a lot of calcium but the dairy propagandists have not told you that the heat of pasteurization kills the dairy calcium phosphatase enzymes necessary for calcium metabolism, causing poor assimilation of the available calcium in dairy products.

Dairy food advertisements also do not tell you that osteoporosis is caused by tobacco acids, soft drink phosphoric acid and excess

31

dietary protein all of which leech the calcium from your bones and teeth; by alcohol which impairs calcium absorption; by caffeine, salt and antacids which cause increased calcium excretion; and by insufficient exercise.

Despite what the dairy industry tells you to sell dairy foods, research clearly shows that you are not able to assimilate as much calcium from dairy products as you might hope, that calcium alone from dairy, other foods and most supplements do not prevent or reverse osteoporosis and that although Americans eat lots of dairy, we still have more osteoporosis in the United States than other countries where less dairy is eaten.

But this is hard to believe when dairy foods are one of your favorite foods. You may have a tendency to believe the dairy propagandists to justify not having to give up the milk, cheese, sour cream, yogurt and ice cream that you love. Therefore, you may want to look the other way when you are advised to STOP EATING DAIRY FOODS.

Did you know that cow's milk is the most common allergen food fed to human babies and adults? Wheat is second. Babies, children and adults cannot properly digest cow's milk, especially when it is pasteurized and homogenized.

In addition to the well known allergic reaction to lactose in dairy, studies at the Department of Genetics and Human Variation in Victoria, Australia show that xenogenic antibodies from non-human species, such as cows and goats, can survive biologically intact any dairy food processing. When eaten, these foreign antibodies can pass through the human gut into the blood as toxins causing allergy problems, weakening and destruction of the immune system and hundreds of diseases caused by systemic toxicity, allergy, and immune dysfunction. Another good reason to feed your baby human breast milk instead of xenogenic milk poisons from cows who are utterly different than human beings, Dolly Parton notwithstanding, pardon the double pun.

Homogenization of milk is a time bomb disaster which fragments dairy fat globules into tiny molecules which resist digestion and enter the bloodstream unaltered causing allergy. The heat of pasteurization also alters the fats in dairy.

The protein casein found in cow's milk is insoluble in water and soluble only in acid, making it very difficult for babies and adults to digest. Consequently, partially digested milk protein is another source of dairy allergens.

After three years of age, most humans quit secreting the enzymes necessary to digest milk and that includes pasteurized or raw cow or goat milk providing yet another reason why we have an epidemic of allergy to dairy foods in our country for those who eat dairy foods all their lives.

Along with an allergy to dairy, wheat and other common food allergens, many people have developed a strong allergy to Establishment doctors and nutritionists and that's why it is a good idea to stay away from them.

In addition to being allergic to dairy, you may be addicted to it. When you do not eat your customary dose of dairy food on time, you start to detoxify from its accumulated poisons stored in every cell in your body. You then experience withdrawal symptoms, excess appetite, jumpy nerves, depression, etc. You are hooked on dairy for which you have an allergy-addiction. Your body craves more dairy to stop the withdrawal pains much like a drug addict detoxifying and withdrawing from drugs making him feel like crawling up the walls to get another fix.

Addiction to dairy is based on physical reactions of stored toxins inflaming and irritating the body on their way out of the body and craving more dairy to stop the cleansing and withdrawal symptoms. Granted, the physical component of dairy addiction is strong. But the psychological addiction is stronger and part of it is a stubborn resistance to give up something you like even when you know it is bad for you.

Calling you an addict may get your goat or cow, make you angry and will hopefully help you stop poisoning yourself and your family with dairy products.

Authors of *The XO Factor*, Drs. Kurt Oster and Donald Ross, have found that the tiny fat molecules broken down by homogenization of milk releases enzyme xanthine oxidase, allowing it to pass through the intestinal wall and into the bloodstream where it does not belong. XO then deteriorates the artery walls and the tissues of the heart causing lesions which the body repairs with calcific plaque, cholesterol, fatty material and scar tissue. Over a period of time, these deposits block the flow of blood causing atherosclerosis and cardiovascular disease.

One-half million people die each year, many unnecessarily, from cardiovascular disease. Dr. Oster says that homogenized milk is one of the major causes of cardiovascular disease in America and the main reason why the U.S. death rate from heart attack and stroke is the highest in the world next to Finland, which has a higher consumption of homogenized milk than the U.S. Pasteurization kills the living enzymes galactase for milk sugar digestion, lipase for milk fat digestion and phosphatase, as mentioned previously, for milk calcium digestion and assimilation which contributes toward causing allergy, free radical producing circulating fats and abnormal calcium deposits in joints and blood vessels.

The U.S. Health Service has set as its standard for milk, 100,000 bacteria per teaspoon after pasteurization. After that the bacteria count keeps climbing if the milk is not constantly refrigerated at 40°F. How many more germs are in your "pasteurized" milk after it travels from the dairy to the store where it sits until you take it home and drink it?

In any case, pasteurization itself does not kill all the germs anyway but it does kill the milk's natural enzyme antibiotics in raw milk which normally would help control the bacteria in natural unprocessed milk products.

An unannounced visit to a commercial dairy will turn you off dairy products permanently. What you will find is that the dairy grounds, equipment and the cows themselves are filthy and diseased. You will find machines which use centrifugal force and strainers to clarify and remove pus, feces and other foreign germ-carrying substances, but not very effectively. You see, all that chemicalized feed, antibiotics, hormones and toxic drugs given to cows to stimulate higher milk production make the cows sick and no amount of heat pasteurization and clarification can clean and cover up dirty milk from dirty, diseased cows or goats.

There is actually less bacteria in raw cow's milk than pasteurized milk because the raw milk companies are required to have better sanitation and healthier cows. But raw milk is not recommended either because once a baby or adult becomes allergic to pasteurized and homogenized milk, they are usually allergic to raw milk from cows or goats.

Pasteurization, then, is without a doubt a flimsy excuse offered by government "health" officials for the sale of dirty milk filled with germs, pus and residues from drugs, antibiotics, hormones and pesticides. Both pasteurization and homogenization of milk are a ruse used by the dairy industry to relax their standards of sanitation, to pass off spoiled milk as fresh and to make more money by extending the shelf life of dairy products.

Let us not forget Dr. Pottenger's famous study outlined in the chapter on children. Cats fed processed milk and meat developed terrible degenerative diseases. The feces from these sick cats was so toxic that it killed the plants near the ground where it was placed for disposal.

It is worth noting that most cheese, yogurt and kefir from regular health food stores are made from pasteurized milk. Most yogurt is again pasteurized after it is made, killing all those healthful, friendly bacteria you want from natural yogurt. Again, pasteurized or unpasteurized yogurt, milk and any other dairy foods are not recommended.

You can fool yourself that skim and low fat milk are good for you. But this is another joke played on dairy lovers because raw whole milk with cream fat contains an anti-stiffness factor which prevents joint stiffness and arthritis. Processed low fat milk with the anti-arthritis factor removed may cause calcific arteriosclerosis, arthritis or calcification of the pineal gland and kidneys.

Dairy industry advertisements intentionally misrepresent low fat milk as promoting good health. It causes bad health and they know it. The real reason for removing cream fat from milk is to sell it separately as an ingredient in thousands of processed foods and they make a fortune doing so all at your expense, financially and health-wise.

Furthermore, animals fed on low fat milk develop testicular atrophy with complete sterility. Skim milk may be a major contributory cause of sterility in an increasing number of human males. Skim milk, anyone?

Do you try to avoid giving up dairy foods by saying, "I don't eat that much dairy"? As it turns out, the dairy lover eats a little cheese almost daily, puts a little milk in coffee or cereal pretty regularly, has cheese pizza once a week or so, eats ice cream once or twice a week and eats a lot of yogurt with the pitiful excuse, "Yogurt is good for me, right?" When all that "little bit" of dairy food is added up over a period of a week, it turns out that he is eating a sufficient amount of dairy to keep him stuffed with mucus and sick.

When it is suggested to the dairy lover that his favorite food may be making him sick, he will often claim that he is healthy despite a history of sinus problems, frequent colds, constipation and other health problems directly caused by eating dairy foods. Until he is ready to eliminate all dairy, the average person will simply avoid nutritional doctors and make repeat visits to orthodox doctors who play the game of avoiding the issue of giving up dairy and other unhealthful foods.

Consequently, the dairy enthusiast may continue to have neck and back pain and health problems directly caused by accumulation of dairy toxins and mucus. He is likely to continue taking drugs or getting chiropractic adjustments to merely alleviate symptoms when he would be better off if he eliminated the dairy which caused his health problems in the first place.

The dairy food, processed food, drug industry and medical monopoly doctors would have you think otherwise but dairy foods are a well established cause of toxicity and mucus, which accumulates all over the body plugging up the eliminative system, wearing down the immune system causing allergy, congestion, inflammation, edema, swelling, muscle contractions, pain and dysfunction all over the body. Your bowels, liver, lungs, kidneys, lymph, sinuses and skin try to eliminate the dairy poisons and mucus. These eliminative organs are precisely the areas that give dairy eaters trouble causing constipation, colds, flu, sinusitis, sore throat, tonsilitis, lung problems, lymph congestion, stubborn infections, skin problems, earache, eye difficulties, and neck, shoulder and low back stiffness and pain.

Keeping in mind that the eliminative organs, especially the lungs and kidneys try to eliminate toxins from dairy, as well as from smoking, coffee, alcohol, drugs, candidiasis, etc., you will understand that back problems are caused by dairy and other poisons. The inflammation and congestion in the lungs and kidneys spread to the corresponding spinal nerves causing nerve inflammatory responses, swelling, spinal muscle contractions, spinal fixation/subluxation, nerve interference, a round robin exacerbation of symptoms periodically, fibrous adhesions of back muscles, progressive degenerative processes, chronic stiffness, arthritis, cancer and so on. SLEEPING ON ABDOMEN COMPOUNDS SPINAL PROBLEMS.

Your Establishment doctor will tell you that this is nonsense but an alternative doctor will understand, help you identify the problem and treat it with natural therapies.

Lung toxicity and inflammation from dairy will therefore cause thoracic vertebrae T2-4 spinous pain in the center of the spine and muscle contractions, stiffness and pain between the shoulders, and in the shoulders, neck and down the arms and hands.

Similarly, kidney toxicity and inflammation from dairy will cause thoracic and lumbar T10-L1 transverse process pain off to the sides of the spine, muscle contractions, stiffness and pain in the low back, sacro-iliac, legs, knees and ankles.

All this from dairy toxins? Yes, and more. The liver becomes inflamed also by dairy toxins causing pain upon palpation of the liver-gall bladder and pain at the liver reflex point between the spine and right shoulder blade. The liver reflex area becomes increasingly inflamed, which adds to the symptoms caused by the nearby inflamed lung place on the spine. This combination of liver reflex point inflammation and lung place inflammation PLUS SLEEPING ON THE ABDOMEN creates a complex of generalized inflammation of the upper back, shoulders, neck and arms causing much stiffness and pain.

Dairy toxins poison and inflame the whole body. The most common food allergy found in inflammatory bowel disease and cancer is dairy (and wheat). Intake of milk fortified with synthetic vitamin D decreases magnesium assimilation and causes osteoporosis. Diet surveys have shown that premenstrual syndrome patients with anxiety, irritability, mood swings and nervous tension related to a depletion of magnesium consume five times more dairy than other PMS subgroups. Magnesium deficiency causes kidney stones and calcifications in other organs and tissues as a result of calcium to magnesium ratio imbalance due to dairy consumption.

The solution? The first step is to make a personal decision to treat your body as the temple of God instead of a garbage dump for dairy poisons. Clean the dairy toxins out of every cell in the body with a good detoxification diet repeated until you have regained your health. Stop eating all dairy foods for the rest of your life.

After you have detoxified the body thoroughly, you might be able to include a little butter to grease baking pans. Most people who are allergic to dairy foods can tolerate a little butter in their diets but it should be limited because, like all free oils, butter can cause indigestion, poor assimilation and constipation.

Eliminate all dairy right away or slowly decrease it to zero. The goal is to eliminate all dairy. Your body will not detoxify and heal until all forms and all amounts of dairy are stopped completely. As explained in the chapter on toxicity and constipation, each cell in your body has stored accumulated toxins from dairy and other foods and bad habits. Even if you limit the amount of dairy consumed, your cells will not release and clean out dairy toxins until you stop eating all dairy products altogether. Ice cream, once in awhile, for example, will signal your cells to continue storing, not releasing dairy toxins. That little bit of milk or cream in your coffee will tell your cells to store dairy poisons.

Cutting down on dairy consumption won't work but when you completely eliminate all dairy in your diet, your cells will then release accumulated dairy toxins. Help neutralize the toxins as they exit the body by taking a series of colonics or enemas along with an herbal laxative once a day for 7 days at least, then one per week and repeat the 7 day cleansing program every 6 weeks. Take lots of vitamin C. This detoxification program is especially helpful when you experience a healing crisis as a result of detoxifying from dairy.

Massage and chiropractic can help soothe and heal the body during the stressful healing and detoxification process.

Sounds like heavy recommendations for withdrawing from drug or alcohol addiction. Drugs and alcohol are worse but withdrawing from dairy addiction can be rough enough because people love dairy so much.

Once you decide to solve your own health problems, it will be easier to eliminate all dairy. When you are ready, try some milk substitutes like almond milk, sunflower seed milk, soy milk, etc. Use cashew spread instead of sour cream, cheese and dips. Order pizza and Mexican food without cheese. Make sure dining-out foods or processed foods do not have dairy in them. Don't let a dairy lover talk you into cheating with him. When depressed, find some good natural food other than dairy to make you feel better.

AFFIRMATION: "I, _____ , love myself and my health and I hearby release, let go and give up all milk, cheese, sour cream, yogurt and ice cream willingly and happily. When offered dairy foods, I express my personal power with love and kindness to those less fortunate souls who love dairy more than they love themselves or me."

DESSERTS

DESSERT: CAKE — FRUIT COBBLER

2 c. cookie crumb base — *see recipe, page 42*
1 c. toasted rolled oats
1 c. chopped walnuts
¾ c. creamed cashews
¼ c. honey or maple syrup
1 tbsp. vanilla
1 tbsp. lemon or lime juice
¼ tsp. sea salt

4 c. prepared fruit
1 c. undiluted frozen apple juice concentrate
1 c. honey or maple syrup
1 tbsp. vanilla
2 tbsp. lemon or lime juice
¼ tsp. sea salt
arrowroot or cornstarch

Preheat the oven to 425°F. Toast the oats in the oven in a baking pan at 425°F, periodically turning them over with a flat spatula until golden brown. Blend ½ c. cashews in just enough water to cream them. Mix the oats, cookie crumbs, nuts, cashew cream, sweetener, vanilla, lemon juice and salt.

Prepare various fruit as follows. Soft tender fruit like peaches, nectarines, fresh apricots, mango, pineapple and berries should be cut into bite size pieces (no need to cut the berries) and briefly cooked in a covered pot without water to remove most of the water. Do not overcook. Heat just enough to remove the water in the fruit and soften them just a little. Save the water from the fruit for the thickener. Apples (green baking apples) should be peeled, cut into bite size pieces, baked in a buttered skillet at 425°F for 20 minutes or until they are softened a little and then sauteed briefly in a little honey. Dried fruit should be steamed to soften them and then sauteed briefly in honey. Papaya can be cut and used as is. Prepare 4 or more cups of fruit and save the water.

For the thickener, blend the water drained from the fruit, 1 cup undiluted frozen apple juice concentrate, 2 heaping tablespoons prepared fruit, 2 tsp. vanilla, 2 tbsp. lemon juice, 2 or 3 table-

spoons arrowroot or cornstarch and ¼ tsp. sea salt. Carmelize
1 cup of honey by cooking it in a pyrex glass pot. Stir it down
when it boils and repeat this until it boils up 3 to 5 times. When
the honey is carmelized, add the blended ingredients and stir
continually until it thickens. Mix the thickener with the prepared fruit. In a buttered pyrex
baking dish, put in half of the rolled oat/cookie mixture. Next pour
in the mixed fruit and thickener and put the remaining rolled
oat/cookie mixture on top and press down and smooth out the top.
Bake at 350⁰F for 20 - 30 minutes. Serve with hot herb tea and
perhaps a frozen dessert made from almond milk. Also good cold.

DESSERT: CAKE — GERMAN PANCAKE

6 eggs or more
1 c. cookie crumb base, skillet bread crumbs or flour
½ c. cashews creamed in a little water
½ c. applesauce, cooked sweet potato, yam,
    squash, pumpkin or raw shredded carrot
1 or 2 tsp. vanilla
½ tsp. sea salt
1 or 2 tsp. baking powder
½ c. raisins
½ c. walnuts
½ c. unsweetened coconut, macaroon or shredded
    extra coconut for bottom of pan and top of cake

Preheat oven to 350⁰F. Butter an iron skillet, Vision skillet or
baking dish and cover the bottom with coconut. In a blender, blend
the eggs, crumbs or flour, creamed cashews, applesauce or
vegetables, vanilla and salt until smooth. Add the baking powder
to the blender and blend very briefly. Stop the blender and add
the raisins, walnuts and coconut and stir by hand or turn on the
blender for a split second to mix only. Pour batter into the buttered
skillet or dish with coconut on the bottom. Put more coconut on
top. Bake at 350⁰F for 30 minutes or until done. Use a knife to
separate the edges and a spatula to separate the bottom and turn
the cake over onto a cloth and cover. Alternative: Omit baking
powder and substitute 2 packages of baker's yeast. Pour into the
skillet or pan and let it rise 2 hours before baking.

DESSERT: CAKE — UNBAKED FRUIT CAKE

4 c. cookie crumb base — *see recipe, page 42*
16 oz. each chopped unsulphured, unsweetened
    dried dates, figs, pineapple and raisins
4 c. chopped walnuts
2 c. unsweetened coconut, shredded or macaroon
3 grated or ground orange rinds
3 tbsp. vanilla
1 c. pineapple juice
1 c. grape juice
3 tsp. cinnamon
2 tsp. allspice
½ tsp. ground clove
1 tsp. sea salt
lots of extra toasted unsweetened shredded coconut
    for the bottom and top

In a very large bowl, mix all of the ingredients except the extra coconut for the bottom and top. If too wet, add more cookie crumbs and if too dry, add more pineapple or grape juice. Mix, knead and press together to form a compact mass. In the oven toast the coconut for the bottom and top and put it in the bottom of 4 or more buttered (butter bottom and sides) casserole dishes or flat plastic containers with covers. Press the dough into the dishes or containers, making sure they are pressed down firm and hard. Sprinkle toasted coconut on top. Place each covered casserole or container in a plastic bag and refrigerate for one week or up to two months. The longer the better the flavor. Marinate periodically with a mixture of honey, vanilla, grape juice, wine or brandy. Take it out slice by slice or place the casserole (but not the plastic containers) in the oven at 425°F for a few minutes only to soften the butter around the edges. Remove from the oven and work with a knife along the sides and turn it upside down on a cloth.

DESSERT: CANDY — CAROB

8 oz. chopped walnuts
2 c. macaroon unsweetened coconut
1 c. raw cashews — ground
½ c. raisins   (cont. next page)

2 tbsp. arrowroot
1 c. honey
½ lemon, juiced
3 tsp. vanilla
½ tsp. sea salt
1 c. toasted carob powder
4 tbsp. lecithin granules or liquid
lots of macaroon unsweetened coconut for bottom
    and top

Preheat oven to 350°F. Butter an 8 x 12 inch flat bottom pyrex dish and cover the bottom with a good amount of coconut. In a large mixing bowl, put the walnuts, coconut and raisins. Carmelize the honey. It is important to have everything ready and to follow the proper order. In a Vita-Mix or strong blender, blend the ground cashews with the honey, lemon juice, vanilla, lecithin and salt. When smooth, add the carob and arrowroot and blend until smooth and hot. Pour into the bowl with the walnuts, coconut and raisins and mix and then put the candy into the dish with the coconut on the bottom. Put more coconut on top and press it down firm. Refrigerate and serve. For a firmer candy, bake in a 350°F oven for 30 minutes. Allow to cool and then cover with a large plastic bag and refrigerate for 8 hours until it sets up. Slice and serve.

DESSERT: COOKIE CRUMB BASE OR CRUST

4 c. wheatless flour — *see bread recipe*
1 - 2 tsp. sifted baking powder
1 tbsp. vanilla
optional: ½ tsp. sea salt, 1 c. honey

Preheat the oven to 425°F. Mix all the ingredients with just enough water to make a cookie batter. Butter a large baking pan, pour in the batter and bake at 425°F for 20 to 30 minutes, until done. Allow to cool. While in the baking pan, cut into small cubes, remove with a flat spatula and store in the freezer until needed.

COOKIE CRUMB CRUST —

3 c. cookie crumbs
1 c. rolled oats (optional)
1 c. ground walnuts, almonds or cashews
1 tbsp. lemon or lime juice   (cont. next page)

1 tbsp. vanilla
¼ tsp. sea salt
a little honey
½ c. macaroon coconut (optional)

Preheat oven to 350°F. Use just enough honey or maple syrup to make the right consistency. Mix all the ingredients, compress and squeeze with your hands to form a compact dough. Butter a pie or baking pan and press dough into the middle of the pan and press down to spread it out on the bottom and sides to the right thickness. Trim off any excess. Poke holes in the crust with a fork to prevent swelling. Bake by itself at 350°F for 15 minutes. Use right away or cool and store in the freezer in the pan covered with a plastic bag until needed.

DESSERT: ESSENTIAL RAW SEED DATE BARS

6 eggs
2 tsp. vanilla
1 c. combination ground raw flax, sunflower,
    pumpkin seeds
¾ c. brown rice or wheat flour
½ c. date sugar
¼ tsp. sea salt
2 tbsp. honey

1 c. honey, carmelized
2 tsp. vanilla
1½ c. chopped dates
½ c. date sugar
little lemon or lime juice
¼ to ½ tsp. sea salt (optional)
1 c. combination ground raw flax, sunflower,
    pumpkin seeds
1 c. chopped walnuts

macaroon coconut

In a blender, mix eggs, vanilla, salt, date sugar, flour, ground seeds and honey and pour into a buttered 8″ x 12″ baking dish with the bottom covered with macaroon coconut. Bake at 425°F for 20 minutes and cool to room temperature.

In a kitchen machine using the bottom blade, chop fresh pitted dates along with ½ cup date sugar. The date sugar helps keep the dates from sticking together during chopping. Carmelize 1 cup of honey by boiling it for several minutes and then add the chopped dates with the date sugar and the vanilla and lemon or lime juice and optional salt. Remove from heat and stir to moisten and soften the dates and date sugar for 15 minutes or longer. In a bowl, mix 1 cup combination ground flax, sunflower and pumpkin seeds and 1 cup chopped walnuts and then pour in the date mixture and mix by hand to a thick paste. Taste test and add more vanilla, lemon or salt to taste.

When the baked bottom is cool, spread the date-seed mixture on top keeping away from the sides. Press down and cover with 2 cups toasted coconut. Press down. Slice into 8 pieces and remove each slice and cut it in half to make a total of 16 pieces. Use the excess toasted coconut to cover the sides of each piece to make it less sticky. Refrigerate and serve with herbal tea.

Essential in the recipe title refers to linolenic and linoleic essential fatty acids which are necessary for health. Flax, sunflower and pumpkin seeds are the highest known sources of these essential nutrients. Flax seed is the richest source of all food sources of linolenic (50 to 60%) and linoleic (15 to 25%) and is a treatment for lowering blood pressure, decreasing platelet stickiness, acne, psoriasis, cancer and other health problems.

DESSERT: PIE — SWEET POTATO AND PINEAPPLE

> 3 c. baked sweet potato
> 1 pineapple, chopped fine
> 1 c. chopped walnuts
> ½ c. honey or maple syrup
> 2 tbsp. vanilla
> 1 lemon or lime, juiced
> ¼ tsp. sea salt
> 1 tbsp. minced ginger or ginger powder
> 1 tsp. allspice
> cookie crumb crust recipe — *see page 42*

Preheat the oven to 425°F. Bake sweet potatoes with the skins for 30 minutes or until done. Check to see if they are done by poking them with a fork. Remove the smaller ones as they are done.

Remove the skins and save them to add to the crust recipe. Mash (do not use blender) the sweet potatoes while warm. It is best to bake the sweet potatoes and make the crust the day before or in the morning so as not to detract your energy from preparing the main course.

Chop the pineapple fine and place it in a pot and cook it over medium heat for about 5 minutes — just enough to cook the excess water out of it. Drain and save the water for another recipe. Carmelize a little honey, add the drained pineapple and cook briefly.

Mix all the ingredients together, taste test and add more seasoning if necessary. Prepare the crust, adding the skins of the sweet potatoes. Put the filling in the crust and bake at 425°F for 20 to 30 minutes. Serve hot or cold.

Alternatives: Add 1 cup macaroon unsweetened coconut to the filling. Top with shredded coconut or creamed cashews with honey, vanilla, lemon and salt. Or top with chopped walnuts sauteed in butter mixed with carmelized honey, vanilla, lemon and salt. Substitutes: kabocha pumpkin, yam, squash or pumpkin.

DESSERT: TREAT — CARMEL POPCORN OR PUFFED BROWN RICE

>   lots of popcorn or puffed or crispy brown rice
>   2 c. finely chopped walnuts
>   1 c. raisins
>   1 c. toasted macaroon coconut (optional)
>   8 - 16 oz. rice or barley syrup
>   ½ c. or more honey
>   2 tsp. vanilla
>   1 - 2 pats of butter
>   ½ tsp. sea salt (optional)

Make some popcorn or bake puffed or crispy brown rice in the oven at 425°F for 10 minutes, stir with a spatula and continue baking until it is more crispy. After baking, the puffed or crispy brown rice will be even softer but when it cools, it will be more crispy than originally. If macaroon coconut is added, toast it first in the oven for 10 minutes, turn with spatula and continue until toasted. Mix the rice or barley syrup, honey, vanilla, butter and salt (optional) in a pot, stir, bring to a boil, stir, reduce or remove from heat to avoid boiling over, bring to a boil again, repeat for a third boil, pour over the popcorn or rice, nuts, raisins and coconut (optional) and mix. Cover the bottom of a large baking pan with toasted macaroon coconut or chopped nuts and seeds, pour in the treat and spread thin. Cool and set up in the refrigerator. Serve individual portions in a bowl and provide tablespoons for anyone who does not want to get his or her fingers sticky. If you like to lick your fingers, lick your left hand fingers, if you are right handed, for sanitary reasons.

DR. DEAL'S DELICIOUS DETOX DIET

The Detox Diet is a permanent, cleansing diet designed to cleanse, rest, nurture and heal your body, mind and spirit daily for the rest of your life. A clean, well-nourished body means a clean, peaceful mind and a clean, joyful spirit.

The detox diet for breakfast and lunch cleanses and rests your body two-thirds of the day and then for dinner nourishes and builds up your body the remaining one-third. The best of two worlds, cleansing and building, and the food tastes good and you have lots of energy during both processes.

For breakfast and lunch, eat cleansing raw fruit and fresh fruit juices or raw vegetables, sprouts, salads, oil-free salad dressing, fresh vegetable juices, some raw seeds and nuts ground or creamed and for dinner eat cooked whole grains, lentils, beans, vegetables and more raw foods, sprouts and salads, dulse, kelp, etc. Once or twice a week, eat fish, eggs, organic beef or poultry. The idea is to eat raw fresh foods for breakfast and lunch and eat cooked food only at dinner along with more raw foods.

Raw foods eaten at breakfast and lunch readily pass through the body requiring little digestion and yet, provide high energy for maximum performance during the workday. Eating only clean raw foods is a form of high energy fasting every day.

Some people may prefer to eat raw foods for breakfast and dinner and eat cooked and more raw foods at lunch for convenience or for some who claim it gives them more energy during the afternoon. For some, eating a raw food lunch makes them feel weak at first because their previous average American diet weakened their digestive systems and they are now not able to digest and assimilate all the nutrients from the raw foods. Eating a cooked food lunch may be good for a breaking in or transitional period until the body is thoroughly cleansed, rested and able to assimilate foods more easily to get the proper nutrition and energy from them. After this trial period, you may want to try eating the raw foods for breakfast and lunch which are more likely then to provide you with all the energy you need.

During the transitional period, if you like, eat a raw food breakfast and for lunch eat a big vegetable salad with seed and lentil sprouts and for more energy add cooked brown rice or millet (served cold) with a good oil-free dressing. Cook the grains the night before; you will find that if you roast the grains in the oven before cooking them, they impart a great nutty grain flavor to the vegetable salad and dextrinized grains are easier to digest. For dinner, in this case, you would eat cooked food with some raw foods.

Another transitional idea is to eat raw fruit for breakfast and for lunch have a vegetable salad and cooked fish and for dinner eat cooked and raw food without more fish, of course. Instead of having fish for lunch every day, try it every other day and then decrease it to once or twice a week. For people used to eating fish or meat every day, this is a good compromise which provides lots of energy.

These modifications during the initial period give you good nutrition, high energy, cleansing, healing and time to get used to the idea of a Detox Diet. After a couple of months, you will have more and more energy, your digestion will improve and you can then try to eliminate the cooked grains or fish from the lunch. On days when you need more energy, add the cooked grains or fish back to your lunch temporarily.

UPON RISING: Start each day saying out loud or to yourself, "Praise God," or "Thank you, Lord," on good days and especially on bad days to replace any negative thoughts and feeliings with positive ones, remembering that the only person blocking God's love and blessings for you is yourself. Your feelings and life circumstances may not be perfect, but God's love for you and your love for Him are perfect. Despite the cold, cruel world and our own dark imperfections, claim victory every morning when you wake up, "Praise God."

As soon as you get up, drink a glass of filtered or distilled water at room temperature, especially on days when you are toxic or out of sorts.

Wait a little while until you are ready and then drink a lemon-flax shake. Grind 2 heaping tablespoons or 1 oz. fresh whole flax seed in a coffee grinder and place in a blender with three ice cubes, 8 oz. water or herb tea (Essiac and flavonoid free radical scavenger formula — see recipe) and blend until smooth, adding more ice cubes if the blender gets the contents warm. Add vitamin C powder and the juice of one freshly squeezed lemon and blend briefly. Variation: also add 1 oz. freshly ground milk thistle seed to detoxify the liver and also perhaps 1 tsp. astragalus powder to build up the immune system.

Flax seed is one of the highest known sources of the omega 3, 6 and 9 essential fatty acids, linolenic, linoleic and oleic used in every metabolic process in the body. Flax seed is wonderful for the skin and hair and it even has a mild laxative effect. Flax should be eaten daily as one of your most important foods promoting overall good health. It is also a specific treatment for cancer and immune deficiency problems. In addition to the flax shake, freshly ground flax seed can be sprinkled on cooked grains and vegetables or on fresh vegetable salads or mixed with applesauce.

Note that fresh lemon juice (not processed or not squeezed the night before and not lime, grapefruit or orange) is the only food which is anionic, or negatively charged. The negative charge and the alkalinity of fresh lemon juice aids the production of bile which is also anionic and alkaline. Without adequate production of bile, we cannot adequately digest our food and get energy from it. 40% bile production, for example, means 40% energy, life and health and 60% fatigue, disease and an early death.

According to the Biological Theory of Ionization put forth by Dr. Carey Reams, we get energy, life and health from the energy created by the foods we eat. Our bodies are cationic or positively charged and almost all foods are cationic except freshly squeezed lemon juice which, along with minerals, especially from vegetables, helps us maintain a proper anion-cation balance necessary for all metabolic functions in the body, including basic digestion and assimilation of food.

You can use pH testing paper (Nitrazine brand, etc. without a prescription from a pharmacy) to test the pH of your saliva and your urine, both of which should be a pH of 6.40. The pH may be a little more acid or lower in the morning as a result of digesting our own acidic fat and protein stores in our bodies during the night. Any deviation, higher or lower than pH 6.40 during the day, means a sharp loss of energy and sickness. Your alternative doctor can help you learn how to achieve the proper anion-cation balance.

MORNING WALK: When possible, get up early enough to take a nice walk each morning after drinking lemon water or a lemon-flax shake to keep physically and mentally fit. Practice deep breathing during the walk and find a good place to stop briefly to do a little stretching. Fast walking is recommended for most people. Running jars the spine and organs and most people cannot tolerate it.

During your walk, pray, meditate and silently say ''Praise God,'' ''Thank you, Lord,'' ''Thank you, Lord, for giving me the challenge of exercise, play, work and relationships to glorify you.'' The next time you have a boring or difficult task in front of you, thank the Lord for it and you will breeze through it more easily. Blessing your energy, your health and your life is effective.

BREAKFAST: About an hour or so after lemon water or the lemon-flax shake, you will be ready for raw whole fruit, fresh fruit juice, a fruit smoothie or fresh vegetable juice. Do not mix fruits and vegetables in the same meal to avoid indigestion. The fruit should be whole and juicy like papaya, pineapple, mango, orange, tangerine, grapefruit, juicy pears, melon (by itself), etc. Juicy fruits cleanse the body much better than drier fruits like banana, apples, dry pears, etc.

One of my favorite fruit smoothies is made by blending 3 to 5 ice cubes, 1 pineapple, 2 papayas, 1 banana and the juice of 4 oranges or a little lemon or lime juice to jazz it up. Avoid fruit smoothies with soy or dairy protein powders which are hard to digest and are frequently allergenic.

Instead of fruit every morning, about half the time try fresh carrot juice or carrot juice mixed with parsley, celery, and other vegetable juice. You will find that fresh vegetable juice vitalizes you and makes you feel better than whole fruit. Both vegetable and fruit juice have lots of living enzymes, vitamins, minerals and nutrients and vegetable juice more so. Fresh vegetable juice has less natural sugar than fruit or fruit juice and is less likely to cause a mild hypoglycemic high blood sugar rush which sometimes happens when eating fruit or drinking fruit juice on certain days.

If you are making a transition to eating more healthful foods, overly stressed, very toxic, ill, in poor health, detoxifying too rapidly or experiencing a hypoglycemia low or high blood sugar imbalance (lightheaded, fatigue, irritable, depressed, etc.) on any particular day or when you have a lot of hard, physical work to do that day, you may not be able to tolerate eating only raw fruit and vegetables on that particular day. You may feel strong the next day and you can then continue the fruit or vegetable juice.

Therefore, on certain days or period of time instead of eating raw foods as usual, you may need for breakfast cooked macrobiotic foods, brown rice, oatmeal, millet or buckwheat perhaps mixed with a little almond or rice milk, dates, raisins and a little brown rice or barley malt syrup. Generally, people like sweetened grains in the morning. Make a big pot full because you may need to eat some periodically throughout the day to keep your strength up. Take it to work with you.

Other possibilites are: baked sweet potato, steamed vegetables or crumbled skillet bread in carrot juice or almond or rice milk.

Avoid processed box cereals and granola which are fun foods for cheating on rare occasions with very little nutrition and granola usually irritates the gastro intestinal tract when eaten more than a couple of days consecutively.

On normal days, eat the recommended whole juicy fruits or drink fresh vegetable juice for breakfast. In general, the healthier you are, the less toxic you are, the better you eat, the fewer bad days you will have and they will occur less frequently as you get healthier and stronger.

DRINK WATER: Between breakfast and snacktime, drink 16 oz. room temperature water. In general, drink 2 to 3 quarts of water a day to aid digestion and elimination. The water should be room temperature filtered or distilled plain or with a little lemon or lime juice for flavor. Approximately 1 hour or 30 minutes before eating, drink 16 oz. of water.

MID-MORNING SNACK: For snacks, eat the same foods you eat for breakfast. To the list, you can add cut raw vegetables, plain without anything on them: carrot, celery, jicama, sunchokes, parsley, etc. Do not eat raw seeds, nuts or dried fruit. Remember, the key word from bedtime the night before to dinner the next day is DETOXIFY with raw fruits and vegetables. On bad days, have a snack of cooked, sweetened grains, which is great cold or warm.

LUNCH: The same as breakfast. Other choices: vegetable salad with lemon juice or dressing with no free oil; cut raw vegetable sticks; avocado by itself plain or with a little dressing or add it to the salad; vegetable salads can be made a little bit more hearty and satisfying by adding avocado, sprouts, shredded raw or pieces of cooked sweet potato or yam; skillet bread plain or with a little nut or seed butter (almond butter, not peanut butter); herb tea; fruit smoothie without protein powder.

Try to get away from the wheat bread and sandwich habit because many people eat too much wheat and this is why they are allergic to it. Substitute wheatless skillet bread or brown rice cakes or crackers but it is best to not eat any bread or cooked food for lunch.

On days when not feeling tops, eat cooked grains for breakfast and lunch to pick you up.

DRINK WATER: Drink another 16 oz. of room temperature water between lunch and dinner and drink another 16 oz. 60 or 30 minutes before snacking or dinner. Don't worry about edema or gaining weight from drinking water. If this happens, it simply means your body is toxic and inflamed and it is retaining excess water to neutralize the high concentration of toxins, to put out the fire of inflammation or you have kidney problems from unhealthful foods and bad habits. The solution is not to avoid water but to detoxify, get the inflammation out of your body and detoxify the kidneys, liver, spleen and blood by eating healthful foods and giving up the bad habits of smoking, alcohol, coffee, medical and street drugs.

MID-AFTERNOON SNACK AND NAP: Same as breakfast, morning snack or lunch. Lie down or put your feet up, meditate or nap for 15 or 20 minutes. A nap any longer can make you groggy the rest of the day. After your nap, stretch a little and have some water or herb tea.

DINNER: Be sure to drink 8 to 16 oz. of water 60 to 30 minutes before eating dinner to help digestion and elimination. Dinner should include cooked brown rice, millet, buckwheat or corn, preferably pre-toasted and dextrinized, combined with a little cooked lentils (easy to digest) or beans (harder to digest). Corn on the cob, corn pasta or baked squash or pumpkin is a nutritious change. Include a steamed or cooked vegetable; raw vegetable salad with lemon juice or dressing with no free oil; dulse or kelp for iodine to keep your thyroid gland happy; herbal tea; and no dessert.

Eat clean fish or organically raised eggs about once or twice a week. The clean fish are mahimahi, halibut, sole, salmon, cod, haddock, bluefish, butterfish, croaker, cusk, grouper, hake herring, kipper, ling cod, mullet, pilchard, pollock, pompano, porgy, red snapper, rose fish, shad, whiting, bass, sardines and trout.

Organically raised beef, lamb, mutton and chicken are acceptable but make sure the meat does not contain residues of antibiotics, hormones, pesticides, drugs and chemicals.

One of the most common mistakes is eating regular chicken in order to stay away from red meat. Chickens nowadays are raised in cramped cages in poorly vented buildings with harmful fluorescent lighting. The chickens never get a breath of fresh air or see the natural sunlight. They are fed processed chicken feed and chemicalized water filled with antibiotics, hormones, growth stimulators, tranquilizers and other drugs to make them grow fat quicker and to help them fight infectious diseases and behavior problems caused by their unhealthful food and living conditions. A large percentage of these chickens have cancer and are unfit for human consumption despite their approval by the Food and Drug Administration.

Eliminate all dairy, free oils, processed foods, soft drinks, candy, junk food, pork, ham, bacon, pork chops, pork roast, sausage, lard, cold cuts, hot dogs, shrimp, lobster, clams, oysters, prawn, scallops, octopus, squid, eel, mackerel, tuna, ahi, ono, catfish, carp, shark, swordfish, marlin and any blood meat or fish containing toxins which can make us sick.

Take any necessary supplements with dinner and lunch. It is best to take them right before eating. Hydrochloric acid tablets should be taken right after meals to aid digestion when needed.

Desserts taste good but most sweet desserts cause weight gain and fruit desserts interfere with digestion. In general, wait two hours after eating any meal before eating fruit, and it is best not to eat fruit or sweets after 3 p.m. to avoid blood sugar imbalances which may cause mood changes, irritability, increased appetite and sleep disturbances. For these reasons, all fruit and sweets should be consumed before 3 p.m.

When you stop eating fruit and sweets at the wrong time, you will notice improvement in your health and more balanced energy levels. When you cheat and eat fruit or sweets again, you may immediately experience the old problems again, especially insomnia.

EVENING SNACK: Same as other snacks but eliminate fruit and sweets to avoid sleep disturbances caused by the blood sugar increasing rapidly and then falling rapidly. Experiment with snacking to determine the best time and the latest possible time you can eat without causing sleep problems, nightmares or getting up in the middle of the night hungry or to go to the bathroom.

Try baked potato slices, brown rice crackers, cut vegetables and popcorn. Fresh carrot juice is very refreshing in the evening and does not seem to interfere with sleep.

When necessary, take an herbal laxative at bedtime.

PRAY: When you are in bed and ready to go to sleep, take the hand of your spouse, if you are married, and if single, hold your right hand over your chest or solar plexus, and say a prayer out loud. On even days, I pray out loud for both myself and my wife and on odd days, she prays.

Don't go to bed angry. It only hurts you and makes things worse. Forgive yourself and your spouse and everyone else for any hurt or wrong done to you. Holding in anger, resentment, disappointment and guilt is your way, not God's.

In our prayers, we claim success in our personal and business affairs in the name of God and we often mention, in a spirit of forgiveness and letting go, any problems or emotional upsets we may have had during the day.

FALAFELS

2 c. dry garbanzo beans
1 c. toasted, hulled sesame seeds
2 tbsp. minced, fresh parsley
¼ tsp. cayenne pepper or 1 tsp. cayenne hot sauce
2 tbsp. cumin powder
½ tsp. garlic
¼ tsp. each turmeric, basil, coriander, marjoram
½ tsp. sea salt
¼ c. cashew spread
juice of 2 lemons
1 tbsp. liquid aminos
2 eggs

1 cup sliced mushrooms

TAHINI SAUCE:
2 c. toasted, hulled sesame seeds
1 c. cashew spread
juice of two lemons
1 tbsp. cumin
dash of cayenne pepper
½ tsp. garlic
½ tsp. sea salt
2 tbsp. minced, fresh parsley

Select, clean, soak overnight, cook the garbanzo beans and grind or chop in a kitchen machine. Preheat oven to 425°F. Add all the ingredients in the top list, adding just enough water to make a thick batter. Taste test and add more lemon juice, salt or spices. Butter a baking pan, cover bottom with extra toasted sesame seeds, pour in batter and bake at 425°F for 25 to 30 minutes. Slice in pan to make bite size pieces and place in a covered pot until needed.

Marinate 1 cup sliced mushrooms in liquid aminos, garlic and a little cayenne pepper and use as a top garnish.

Prepare the tahini sauce by blending or mixing with water all the tahini sauce ingredients except the parsley which is mixed in with the sauce after it is made. Taste test and add more seasoning to your own taste. Add just the amount of water for the consistency that you like.

Heat pita bread, unleavened griddle bread or taco shells, add the falafels and tahini sauce and top with the marinated mushrooms and a little chopped lettuce and salsa if you like.

FISH

FISH CAKES

4 - 6 pieces fresh or frozen white ocean fish
2 c. skillet bread or whole grain cracker crumbs
1 c. toasted, hulled sesame seeds
1 c. minced celery and/or green pepper
2 - 3 eggs
2 tbsp. lemon juice
2 tsp. herbal seasoning
1 tsp. sea salt
¼ tsp. cayenne pepper

Bake fish at 425°F until done, in an oiled skillet or baking pan. Cool, remove any dark parts or bones and then mince into small pieces. In a mixing bowl, stir all the ingredients, adding just enough egg to form patties. Taste test and add more seasoning if necessary. Freeze extra uncooked cakes on a cookie sheet with waxed paper, bag, store in freezer. To serve, bake at 425°F in an oiled skillet or baking pan for 15 minutes. Turn over and bake another 5 or 10 minutes. Do not overcook to avoid drying them out. Serve plain or covered with walnut gravy or cashew spread. Great as hot or cold leftovers for sandwiches, bag lunches, picnics or camping and good for those who normally don't like fish.

FISH STEW

4 - 6 pieces of fresh or frozen white ocean fish
4 potatoes
4 stalks chopped celery
1 sliced zucchini
3 thinly sliced carrots
1 chopped green pepper

(cont. next page)

1 bunch minced parsley
5 fresh tomatoes or 28 oz. ready cut, peeled
   tomatoes
1 lemon, juiced
½ tsp. garlic powder or granules
¼ tsp. cayenne pepper
2 tsp. herbal seasoning
1 tsp. sea salt
liquid aminos to taste

Bake the fish at 425º F in a skillet or baking pan until done. Cool, cut into bite size pieces and set aside. In a large pot, boil 4 cups of water. Add cubed potatoes and cook until done, stirring often to avoid sticking. Add all of the ingredients and taste test to add more seasoning to your own taste. Cook until the vegetables are barely done. Serve as is or thicken soup with cashew spread, creamed coconut or potato flakes or powder. Remove a little liquid, add the thickener, stir until smooth, add it back to the stew and stir. Add just enough water to make it the right consistency. Serve as is or add a little butter for taste and serve with rice or millet. Great for those who usually don't like fish.

FREE RADICAL PATHOLOGY AND CHELATION THERAPY

Free radical pathology and its treatment, chelation therapy, are the two most significant medical discoveries in this century as equally important as the discoveries of bacteria and antibiotics and the theory of systemic toxicity and detoxification.

Why don't you know about free radicals and why isn't chelation therapy covered by your insurance policy? The patent for EDTA chelation has expired, thereby offering no profit incentive for the medical drug "discoveries" which provide billions of profits each year for the past 70 years for the medical Establishment. In a nutshell, orthodox medical doctors will try to persuade you not to worry about free radical pathology and not to get chelation therapy. You will be told: the free radical and chelation theories are unproven quack theories; free radicals are automatically controlled by the body with superoxide dismutase enzymes to prevent damage; polyunsaturated oils are good for you; chelation therapy can overwhelm kidney function and kill you.

This type of programmed disinformation from orthodox medical doctors across America protects the medical monopoly and can add your own family members and friends to the death statistics of over one million people who die each year from cardiovascular disease and one-half million who die from cancer, mostly unnecessarily.

"One therapy which both prevents death from heart attack and cancer should be enough to win the Nobel prize for those who practice and advance it," wrote Mark Lane in the Spotlight newspaper, October 30, 1989. He continued, "At the same time, it constitutes the greatest threat to the medical Establishment — which thrives on open heart surgery, the No. 1 income provider for hospitals in the United States, and for those who have dined out quite luxuriously for decades on the 'incurable' cancer epidemic.''

Free radicals are highly reactive molecules and molecular fragments with an unpaired electron in an outer orbit causing them to be very unstable and to react quickly with any substance or chemical in their vicinity within the body. Each reaction creates a cascade of more free radicals in a multiplying effect.

When controlled within the mitochondria of each cell, free radicals release useful energy, kill invading bacteria and detoxify chemicals, medical drugs, street drugs, environmental pollutants, rancid fats, etc.

Ozone (Oxygen 3), a form of oxygen, used in ozone therapy produces a beneficial type of free radical activity which super-oxygenates the blood and tissues and destroys disease, according to Anglo-American Research. See chapter on ozone therapy.

Outside the cell where they can multiply a millionfold, free radicals become a type of internal radiation which disrupts cellular membranes; causes cell membranes to leak out and lose cellular chromium, which is a cause of adult onset diabetes and to lose cellular potassium and magnesium and allows the influx of sodium and calcium, which are an important cause of hypertension; inhibits enzymes; scars connective tissue; ages the skin; creates abnormal calcium deposits; decreases the antioxidant role of the good type of cholesterol; strips the protective layers surrounding nerves; increases undesirable mucopolysaccharide breakdown products, lipofuscin, ceroid and melanin; and causes mutagenic damage to the genes and chromosomes, which can cause cancer.

The damage from free radical pathology is cumulative and progressive if the rate of free radical production proceeds unchecked. Eventually, the body's natural defenses are overwhelmed. Inevitably, the body cells, tissues, organs and glands deteriorate and degenerate into a state of disease.

Neither your Establishment doctor nor yourself can wish away the destructive physiological effects of free radicals which cause a wide spectrum of cell damage, inflammatory disorders, circulatory disease and malignant mutations, which in turn lead to atherosclerosis, hypertension, heart disease, stroke, brain ischemia, spinal cord and nerve injury, senility, dementia, Alzheimer's disease, premature aging, wrinkling of the skin, arthritis, cataracts, macular degeneration, multiple sclerosis, cancer and many, many more degenerative diseases — most of which are caused by the very foods, habits and medical drugs and treatment promoted by the medical Establishment.

Dietary fats, primarily those polyunsaturated vegetable oils which you think are healthful foods, are in fact, the leading sources of pathological free radicals. Polyunsaturated fatty acids combine with atmospheric oxygen, creating fatty free radicals called lipid peroxides that attack the walls of blood vessels, ultimately causing atherosclerosis and cardiovascular disease, the most common cause of death in the United States.

Lipid peroxides and other free radicals from dietary fats or stored excess body fat or from peroxidation of lipoprotein cell membranes block the synthesis of good prostacyclin prostaglandin; allows bad thromboxane prostaglandin to build up blood platelet and a network of fibrin and small thrombi clots along the walls of the blood vessels; the clots trap leukocytes and red blood cells, which break down and produce an explosive increase in free radical oxidative damage of good cholesterol and cell membranes; the high concentrations of free radicals cause genetic mutation and cell multiplication, which form atheroma tumors in the wall of the blood vessel; as the atheroma enlarges, it dies inside and attracts calcium deposits, which further harden the walls of the blood vessels, causing atherosclerosis and arteriosclerosis; the atheroma tumors, accumulating platelets and fibrin restrict blood flow, which produces anoxia or lack of oxygen, which produces more free radical pathology; when a blood vessel becomes approximately 75% blocked, stress or overeating can release a blood clot or cause an abrupt spasm and complete blockage of a blood vessel, causing a heart attack or stroke.

For those patients lucky enough to survive, an orthodox doctor would provide emergency treatment and then prescribe drugs to thin the blood, relax the blood vessel walls, reduce hypertension, etc. and he might recommend bypass surgery.

Medical drugs and surgery only treat the symptoms, not the cause, of free radical pathology and three major studies show that bypass surgery does not prolong the life of the patient. But what about treating the cause of cardiovascular disease by eliminating the free radicals and the source of more free radicals?

The main sources of free radical pathology are cold- or heat-pressed polyunsaturated vegetable oils, oil salad dressing, margarine, mayonnaise, vegetable shortening, lard, fats and foods containing hydrogenated oils, such as baked goods, candy, chocolate and chips; anoxia or lack of oxygen from atherosclerosis explained above, smoking cigarettes or street drugs, not breathing deeply and lack of exercise; radiation from unnecessary x-rays; atherosclerotic released ionized iron and copper; aluminum toxicity from food additives, antacid tablets and powders, cosmetics, antiperspirants, bentonite clay and aluminum cookware; fluoridated water or medication which increases aluminum uptake; cadmium toxicity mainly from tobacco smoke and polluted drinking water; complex hydrocarbons in smog and pollution; drinking wine, beer and any alcohol which produces tremendous amounts of free radicals and also pickles the body with acetaldehyde, which is similar to the embalming fluid, formaldehyde; pesticides and herbicides; and chlorine and fluoride in drinking water.

Free radicals themselves create more free radicals exponentially, much like a snowball rolling down the hill getting bigger and bigger. Once the free radicals exceed the control threshold of superoxide dismutase, they increase in large numbers, causing more damage. This process can be controlled by eliminating the major sources of free radicals and by receiving treatment to neutralize the existing free radicals.

The primary treatment for free radical pathology is chelation therapy administered by a medical doctor or osteopath to improve metabolic and circulatory function by removing toxic metals and metallic ions from the body, such as lead, cadmium, aluminum, copper and iron, thereby removing the primary sources of free radical pathology. The amino acid, EDTA, a chelating agent which attracts and binds only certain metals and metallic ions, is administered intravenously in the arm using a tiny needle.

A good mineral and trace mineral supplement is recommended during intravenous or oral chelation and should include kelp and alfalfa and alfalfa, barley green or wheat grass juice concentrate. And, of course, it is important to improve the diet and remove free radical source foods and bad habits. Note that after chelation, take mineral supplements for two weeks and stop for two weeks and continue on and off minerals to prevent accumulation in joints and in the form of gall and kidney stones.

Thirty or more infusions well spaced over a period of time may be necessary to slowly remove the unwanted ions to neutralize or prevent free radical damage. The American College of Advancement in Medicine recommends the slow drip infusion method to allow the kidneys to slowly detoxify the EDTA and metallic ions. Patients are examined and tested for pre-existing kidney damage or disease to determine if the kidneys are healthy enough to withstand the stress of chelation therapy. Properly administered, chelation even improves kidney function.

Many patients improve during chelation therapy and some patients have a three-month delay in achieving full benefit after chelation is discontinued. This delay has been widely reported by chelation doctors.

Ozone therapy, hydrogen peroxide, dioxychlor, Aerox, oxygen therapy with exercise, hyperbaric oxygen raises oxygen levels in ischemic tissues; stimulates the free radical scavenging superoxide enzymes; improves blood flow; helps to kill disease-causing organisms, especially anaerobic bacteria; stimulates ingrowth of new blood vessels to ischemic areas; and protects the fatty insulating sheaths surrounding nerve tracts in the brain and spinal column from free radical damage, relieving symptoms of stroke, senility, multiple sclerosis and spinal cord injury.

Since dietary fat and oil are a primary source of free radicals, they should be restricted to 15 to 20% of total daily calories and taken in the whole natural state and not in the form of free liquid or hydrogenated oils. Eliminate all white flour, white pasta, white rice and sugar which have had all the trace minerals removed. Eggs cooked, boiled and poached with the yolk still intact produces fewer free radicals than scrambling or adding them to baked goods. Drink only pure filtered or distilled water without any fluoride and chlorine. Do not ingest aluminum in processed foods, table salt, drugs, antacids, cosmetics and antiperspirants and do not cook with aluminum cookware. Eliminate alcohol, tobacco, street drugs and unnecessary medical drugs which cause free radical pathology.

Walking for 30 minutes once or twice weekly and vigorous aerobic exercise helps control free radical damage by improving circulation, increasing oxygen intake, and detoxifying the body. Exercise induced lactate accumulation in the tissues has some beneficial chelating properties.

Nutritional antioxidant supplements to neutralize free radicals should include vitamins C and E, zinc, beta carotene and superoxide dismutase, catalase and gluthione peroxidase enzymes in standard doses. But did you know that the herb ginkgo and silymarin from milk thistle seed have many natural antioxidants and free radical scavengers which are more potent than other antioxidants?

Ginkgo, as a major free radical scavenger, has demonstrated effectiveness in the treatment of the circulatory system by its activities of vasodilation, enhanced ATP synthesis, increased glucose uptake, inhibition of platelet aggregation and modulation of calcium flux. Ginkgo has been used effectively to prevent and treat stroke, tinnitus, vertigo, impotency and premature aging.

Silymarin inhibits free radicals which cause most liver damage and also stimulates liver protein synthesis, prevents depletion of glutathione induced by alcohol and other liver toxins, inhibits the liver damaging action of leukotrienes and inhibits prostaglandin synthesis during inflammation.

Treatment for free radical pathology should therefore include milk thistle and ginkgo in clinical doses recommended by naturopathic doctors, medical doctors and chiropractors. Also take blueberry (vaccinium myrtillus), quercetin (a form of rutin flavonoid) and hawthorne (crataegus oxyacantha).

The last chapter can refer you to an alternative doctor for herbs, chelation, ozone and oxygen therapies proven effective in neutralizing and reversing the effects of free radical pathology.

How many of the one and a half million lives of those dying from cardiovascular disease and cancer each year could have been saved in the past and how many could be saved in the future, if orthodoxy would release its tentacles strangling the alternative health movement?

GRAINS: THE STAFF OF LIFE

Grains are a wholesome addition to the diet, the most common source of starch and the least expensive source of calories in most parts of the world. A grain is basically a seed with three parts: the germ, the sprouting part, which contains vitamins, proteins and oils, vitamin E for example; the endosperm or starcy bulk of the grain; and the bran contains minerals, fiber, some vitamins and protein.

As you can see, grains are a nutritious living organism capable of germinating plant life and should be eaten fresh and whole to preserve their nutrients. Therefore, it is best to use fresh whole grains and to freshly grind whole grains to make flour and refrigerate it right away and freeze the flour when storing it.

Wheat, rye, barley, oats contain gluten, a hard to digest protein, which tends to accumulate in the colon, causing toxic by-products which poison and inflame the colon and sexual organs causing toxicity, inflammation, degeneration, allergy, prostate problems and problems with the ovaries, uterus, vagina, menstruation, fertility, etc. This does not mean that gluten grains are not good for you but in the United States, the average person tends to eat too much wheat bread, processed food containing wheat or gluten based meat substitutes. The gluten meat substitutes are especially hard to digest and usually contain many processed additives and chemicals making the product very unhealthful, toxic and a very common food allergen. In general, enjoy wheat, rye, barley and oats in moderation and make an effort to use a variety of these grains instead of eating too much wheat alone to avoid a wheat allergy, which is one of the top food allergens since we tend to eat more wheat than we should because it is so conveniently available and tasty.

Brown rice is an excellent grain, well balanced and, while it does not contain a lot of protein, it is a good quality. Wehani brown rice can be easily sprouted before cooking and sprouting helps convert long chain starches into more easily digested shorter chains. White polished rice should be avoided. Polishing rice removes the bran and improves digestibility but it removes most of the minerals and vitamins. Dextrinizing and hydrolyzing the brown rice improves its digestibility and is a better alternative to polishing the rice.

Millet is a wonderful, light grain, so easy to digest and great in the morning, for lunch or the evening meal. It is the most alkaline grain and is considered yang since it is small and compact. In the United States, we eat the bullrush type, also called pearl millet, and other countries eat sorghum and finger millet.

Millet will get mushy unless it is toasted, and therefore should be toasted in the oven before cooked in water. Millet has to be cooked just right. Otherwise, it is either too hard or too soft and falls apart. It has to be pre-toasted, cooked in water, covered and allowed to sit and fluff up and stir as little as possible to avoid breaking it down but if it crumbles, add it to vegetable soup or bread recipes.

Buckwheat is a nutritious grain (technically not a grain but a fruit) not related to wheat and is usually toasted, called kasha or buckwheat groats, which means the outer shell has been removed and the buckwheat toasted. Add toasted buckwheat to other cooked grains, but it cooks very quickly since it has already been toasted unless you buy the raw groats. Place ½ cup buckwheat groats in 1 to 1½ cups boiling water, cover, remove from heat and let it sit for about 10 minutes to soften. Add to vegetable soup or cooked brown rice, millet or oats or any combination of these grains. Serve with almond milk, brown rice or barley syrup and dates or raisins. Or add cooked buckwheat to bean sauce. Buckwheat is a little dry to eat by itself.

Pre-toasting millet, brown rice and grains helps to dextrinize carbohydrates in grains to shorter chain dextrins which are much easier to digest and sweeter to the taste. And then cooking the pre-toasted grains in water helps to hydrolyze the grain, filling it with water and making it fluff up and also helps to break down the bran covering — all of which make it much more easy to digest. Improperly cooked grains with long starch molecules can enter and block the bloodstream as it normally flows through such vital areas as the brain, kidneys and bones. Longer cooked grains, especially when pre-toasted, dextrinized and hydrolyzed, break down these long starch molecules, making it more easily digested and does not block blood circulation and cause related health problems.

Take care in pre-toasting the grain that you do not scorch or burn it which degrades the proteins, fats and carbohydrates into carcinogens. Toast to a golden brown and it should smell nutty and aromatic, but if it smells scorched or burned, you might discard it and start again.

The most convenient method is to toast a 2 lb. bag of grain, meal, grits or flour by placing it in a baking pan; baking it in a 350° F oven until golden brown; set a timer for 15 minutes; check and turn over with a flat spatula; continue baking; set the timer at 10 minute intervals until done; cool; store in refrigerator and use as needed. Rice usually takes 60 to 90 minutes to pre-toast and millet only about 20 to 30 minutes. Meal, grits and flour take only about 15 to 30 minutes.

Pre-toasting is the first step and an appropriate long cooking time completes the dextrinization process of grains (breaks down the long starch molecules) and also hydrolyzes it (fills it with water and fluffs it up).

To lengthen cooking time after cooking the grains initially, they can be added to other recipes and cooked again with them to ensure proper dextrinization. For example, place cooked grains in water and vegetable broth and cook for an hour or so and then add vegetables, seasoning, etc. and cook until ready. Cooked grains can be added to breads, corn breads, etc. See Bread. Order *Eat For Strength Oil Free, A Vegetarian Cookbook*, $9.45 includes postage, by Agatha Thrash, M.D., Uchee Pines Institute, R. 1, Box 443, Seale, AL 36875-9124, telephone (205) 855-4708 for great recipes.

It is recommended that you purchase a 10 cup electric rice cooker/warmer. Select the model with the warmer to keep the rice warm after it is cooked. All models on the market now have aluminum pots which should be avoided but you will not find one without an aluminum pot. Therefore, buy the oversize 10 cup model to allow you to put a pyrex glass or stainless steel pot inside the aluminum pot. The method is simple. For brown rice (not pre-toasted), put water inside the aluminum pot and place the glass or steel pot with rice and more water inside the aluminum pot. The proportions are as follows: For 1 cup rice, put 1½ cups water in the aluminum pot and also 1½ cups water in the glass or steel pot. For 1½ cups rice, put 2 cups water in the aluminum pot and 2 cups water in the glass or steel pot and so forth. In this way, you can enjoy the convenience of an electric rice cooker without the danger of aluminum poisoning. Use a heavy duty electric timer to have the cooked rice ready when you come home and it keeps for 1 or 2 hours in the warmer.

It is best to pre-toast the rice or millet as part of the dextrinization process. For pre-toasted rice, add 1 cup pre-toasted rice and 1½ cups water to the stainless steel or glass pot and 1½ cups of water to the aluminum pot in the rice cooker and cook. For pre-toasted millet, 1 cup pre-toasted millet and 2 cups water in the glass or stainless steel pot and only 1 cup water in the aluminum pot. Using this method, the rice or millet will cook in the rice cooker for about 20 or more minutes. For longer cooking time, add more water.

SEASONING OPTIONS:

Generally, add liquid aminos, toasted hulled sesame seeds, cayenne pepper and/or garlic to all options below, if desired after the grains have been cooked.

1. Add the following possibilities: rosemary, sage, thyme; cumin; Dr. Deal's herbs; etc.
2. Add various chopped vegetables sauteed in liquid aminos and thinly sliced raw carrots.
3. Add peeled, minced, raw burdock root (gobo).
4. Add various greens sauteed in liquid aminos.
5. Add cooked millet, buckwheat or rolled oats.
6. Add cooked butter beans, lima beans or lentils.
7. Add cooked wehani brown rice or wild rice.
8. Add chopped almonds, walnuts or other nuts.

9. Add cooked noodles, scrambled eggs, minced leek, cooked green peas, sauteed chopped greens, peeled minced burdock root (gobo), cayenne pepper and liquid aminos.

RICE: RICE SALAD

Pre-toast and cook brown rice, cool and add raw salad greens, chopped raw vegetables, sliced ripe or stuffed green olives, bean, lentil and seed sprouts and any other vegetables. Cooked vegetables can also be added for a change of pace.

Serve with salad dressing, cashew spread, a little liquid aminos and add a little water if more moisture is needed.

RICE: SPANISH RICE

Pre-toast and cook rice and add the following.

Make a sauce of tomato sauce, salsa, sea salt, liquid aminos, garlic, cayenne pepper, cumin, lemon or lime juice and Spanish herb mix, Italian herb mix or a combination of oregano, basil and thyme. Taste test and add more ingredients until you like the taste. Heat the sauce briefly or you can simmer it longer at low heat, stir often and add water if necessary.

In a bowl, mix:

chopped green pepper
chopped, raw tomato and/or ready cut peeled
   tomatoes
sliced ripe olives
minced leek
whole kernel raw corn or thawed frozen corn

Mix the cooked rice, vegetables and sauce. Taste test and add more salt, salsa, cumin or lemon or lime juice to make it just the way you like it.

MILLET

For breakfast or anytime, sweeten cooked dextrinized millet with nut-seed milk with honey, vanilla, salt and add chopped dates or raisins and pieces of cooked sweet potato and add water to make it as thin or thick as you like.

Add cooked dextrinized millet to soups, other cooked grains, bread recipes and cool it and add to vegetable salads.

OATMEAL

Rolled oats stored in nitrogen, available in health food stores, are better than rolled oats and quick rolled oats found in super-markets. After opening, store in refrigerator. Cooked oats can be added to cooked rice, millet and buckwheat and also bread recipes. Place pre-toasted rolled oats in a pot with water and cook. Serve with the following choices: honey, chopped dates, raisins, nut-seed milk, pieces of cooked sweet potato or organic apple juice.

GRAVY — WALNUT GRAVY

1 cup walnuts
3 cups pure water
½ tsp. garlic powder
¼ tsp. cayenne pepper
½ tsp. sea salt
dash of liquid aminos
1 tsp. rosemary/sage/thyme combination
2 tbsp. arrowroot powder

Blend all ingredients in a blender until smooth. Taste test and add more seasoning if necessary. Cook in a saucepan over low to medium heat stirring until gravy thickens. Serve over corn bread dressing, mashed potatoes, casseroles, fish cakes, tofu burgers, grains or vegetables.

HEALING THE WHOLE PERSON — BODY, MIND AND SPIRIT

THREE STEPS TO HEALING:

STEP 1:   Releasing and the decision to get well

STEP 2:   Nurture, cleanse and heal the whole person

STEP 3:   Wellness and repeat treatment

HEALING STEP 1: Releasing and the decision to get well

The decision to give up sugar, free oils, dairy, white flour, junk foods, smoking, alcohol, coffee, street and medical drugs, and following through on a complete health treatment program, can be a lonely, frightening experience like walking into a room of hostile strangers with no help in sight because deep down you may have a fear of failure and fear of rejection and perhaps a sense of hopelessness that you simply cannot and will not be able to do everything you want to do to get well.

It is fair to say that 95% of us do not want to change to a better lifestyle or take responsibility for our own health. Most of us have somehow given up hope in ourselves and lost the will to live fully to our maximum potential, preferring the easy way of eating favorite foods and continuing smoking, alcohol and street drugs which make us sick; thinking, believing, feeling and doing what is mostly habit and not that good for us; and taking medical drugs for immediate relief despite the side effects and lack of effectiveness in curing our health problems.

Evaluating and correcting your psychological resistance to wellness is a step by step process much like giving up smoking, for example. Some people prefer to gradually stop smoking and some prefer to stop cold turkey. Likewise, some people prefer to jump right into an intense program of health and self-improvement while others take one little step at a time. And it takes some people many hurtful years before they are able to take a close look at themselves, their problems and their resistance to improvement.

A new more healthful diet and lifestyle is like a meal offered to you. You can choose to take only a bite of the food (for thought) prepared for you or you can eat the entire meal (adopt the whole health program) depending upon how hungry (needful) you are. In either case, as a result of overeating unhealthful foods (excesses, self-abuse, stress), your digestive system (your psyche and spirit) may or may not be strong enough (are you strong enough and ready?) to digest and assimilate (accept) the nutrients (knowledge) and eliminate the waste (letting go). In time, after many false starts, failures (life as it is for all of us) and finally some progress (grace), your digestive system (your psyche, spirit and will to live) will improve, providing better digestion and assimilation (acceptance, understanding) and better elimination (letting go).

In this spirit of seeking and love, look over your diet, habits, lifestyle and health as painful and rewarding as it may be for you to look at yourself. If you do not want to take a look at any resistance to wellness now, try when you are ready.

Do you need the discipline, knowledge, courage and strength necessary to get well and to give up unhealthful foods, bad habits, negative attitudes and a destructive lifestyle? Have you given up on life and God and isn't that why you are sick or not the person you want to be?

Perhaps the following affirmations and prayers will help you feel closer to God and less alone in your decision to start and work through a good health program.

AFFIRMATIONS AND PRAYERS:

Step One in my healing program is opening my heart and my life to God as His creation. I know that God knows everything about me and that He loves me as His child in spite of my weaknesses. I accept God's love and authority in my life and my rewards are love, happiness, peace, joy, freedom, success and good health.

• • • • •

In the name of Almighty God, I surround myself and my loved ones with God's love and power and His armor so only that which is good and necessary can enter and all else return with love to whence it came not only for my own protection but for all who see it or come into contact with it will be drawn to God and healed, mentally, emotionally, physically and spiritually.

• • • • •

In the name of God, I ask that you bless me and bless this food to nourish my body which is your temple. I claim success in taking responsibility personally for my health and to eat only those foods which promote my wellness. I practice only good habits. I take charge of my life. I am strong willed. I am disciplined in my thoughts, emotions and actions. And I do all of this not to glorify myself but to glorify you, Almighty God. Above all, I love You, God, I love myself and everyone, friend or foe, as you love each one of us. I open my heart to you and I eat only the natural food you created for all of us, your children. (Note: change to ''us'' and ''we'' when more than one are praying together.)

• • • • •

In the name of God and the Holy Spirit, divine love is doing its perfect work in me and through me now. I rest and relax in the love of God and I claim your perfect healing, body, mind and spirit. I claim love, discipline, forgiveness, joy, success, prosperity and health in your name, Almighty Father.

• • • • •

When I think about God and who I am in Him, I feel great, safe, confident and loved. But when I worry about myself, my weaknesses and my problems without Him and I could kick myself and I do, I feel terrible, afraid, alone and unloved. I do these mean things to myself and those around me and I could hate myself for doing them and I do, because I go temporarily stupid and forget that when I think about God and who I am in Him, I feel great, safe, confident and loved.

• • • • •

When you face, pass by or think about any person who harbors ill will towards you, look him or her in the eye or in your thoughts and without moving your lips silently say, ''God bless you, _____ .''

Look in a mirror into your eyes and smile into them and into your heart silently saying, "I, _____ , love myself as God loves me. I am a disciplined and obedient child of God who rewards me with love, compassion, joy, prosperity and health. I bless and release all of my problems, emotional blocks and attachments into God's loving and all powerful hands for His analysis and His solutions. I forgive myself, my spouse, mother, father, brothers, sisters, family, friends, associates, superiors, subordinates, neighbors, clerks, policemen, attorneys, judges, doctors, teachers, pastors, politicians, foes and everyone. I am doing something right. I express my personal power with only love and compassion.''

• • • • •

When troubled or not feeling grounded, look into a mirror, look deep into your eyes into who you are and smile. Silently say, "I protect myself and my loved ones with the love, wisdom and power of God at my side." Look more deeply into your eyes into your very soul and smile with the confidence and comfort of a child of God. Look more deeply into any negativity, anger and hate and smile as you turn it over to God and let it go. Look ever more deeply into your eyes into all the love in you and through Jesus Christ and smile. Smile into your eyes and see your eyes themselves smile and come to life. Feel the smile and love move to your eyelids and then to your face, heart, arms, legs and every cell in you. Look into your eyes deeply and say, "God bless me, _____ , and my foolish negativity, anger, hate and revenge" and smile as you place it in His hands. Look into your eyes and feel the love in you and through our Lord and Savior and feel His love and protection in you and around you and smile.

• • • • •

An interesting note about smiling. Closely observe the eyes of the person who is talking to you or someone else in person or on television to watch for the smile reflex. The person will automatically smile just a hint of a smile in the eyes only or it may spread to the face or you can hear an off-note in the voice when he is lying. You can train yourself to know when a person is lying or not. In some cases, the person may be able to hide it although you may still be able to pick it up intuitively.

Use any brightly colored photograph or painting or order 8 x 8'' cards with colored designs, no. 725 Universal Logos $5 or no. 799 set of sixteen cards $40 from Arica Institute, 150 Fifth Avenue, Suite 912, New York, NY 10011, telephone (212) 807-9600 and include $5 postage. Drink some fresh carrot juice or fruit juice to get your energy up, prepare a peaceful and undisturbed environment. Sit in front of another person with the photograph or card in between laying on top of your knees and the other person's knees. Fix your gaze and stare without moving your eyes except to blink at one color only around the edge or perimeter of the photograph or card. Remember to relax and breathe regularly and deeply. Continue staring for 3 to 5 minutes. The longer the better until your eyes begin to fatigue. Move to the next color and stare until the color starts to visually shift, change figure and ground, becomes iridescent, mixes with the surrounding colors, etc. Continue to breathe deeply and stay relaxed and focused. Move on the the next color and so on until you reach the center. Try blinking or slightly squinting to create other visual effects. From time to time, you will feel like smiling, which is great, but concentrate and do not move your eyes. After you have reached the center, then look directly into the other person's left eye and stare deeply into it with courage, love and compassion silently saying, "God bless you, _____ " and continue for 10 minutes or longer until you see, feel and intuit a white light coming from your eyes going into the other person's left eye and a white light coming from his or her eyes coming into your left eye. Silently say, "God, I thank you and praise you," and to the other person say, "God bless you,_____ and I send you my love and God's love."

• • • • •

Alone or with others, bless yourself and everyone and everything around you in the name of God. Unplug the telephone, burn incense, play soft music of temple bells, harp, intonation, Gregorian chant or gospel music. Hold and periodically ring a little bell as the spirit moves you. In a nice room or area outside, stand and walk ever so slowly or lightly slide your feet slowly in slow motion as if in a sea of honey and fragrant flowers. Slowly move your arms in rhythm with your legs all in slow motion, relaxed and feeling wonderful — sort of like doing tai chi. As you glide around, slowly move your head and eyes looking at the beauty of everyone and everything around you. Appreciate the beauty, the light, the shadows, the sparkle, the aroma, the music, the air, the sweetness and love. Ring, ring, ring the bell. Walk, slide, glide in slow motion in honey and silently say, "God bless you" to everyone and everything you see, hear, feel, intuit and smell and feel the softness and love in you and around you. Explore new areas lightly flying slowly as the slowest slow motion turtle for more excitement and magic in you and around you. God loves me. Ring, ring, ring the little bell, tingle, tingle, tingle all over. I love God and all His creation.

• • • • •

Prepare the perfect relaxed environment for yourself or a group. Sit or lie down. Close your eyes and recall the most beautiful, highest, most wonderful experience of euphoria, love, happiness and peace in your whole life. Bring it back to your memory and consciousness. Feel it. Feel the warmth, love and vibration in your body just as it was in the original experience. Record it in your mind. Open your eyes and savor the feelings you have. Open your mind to the following idea. Recall that same experience at any time by simply closing your eyes and allowing yourself to remember and feel all those wonderful feelings. Try it. Close your eyes and recall that experience. When you have, open your eyes. Now close your eyes and recall the experience even more quickly and when you have, open your eyes. Consider the possibility that time is only a concept which you could use to your advantage or disadvantage. Consider the possibility of recalling the experience even more quickly by closing your eyes as quickly as a blink. Try it. Blink and immediately recall the experience. Consider also that you do not have to even blink or close your eyes to remember, recall and feel the experience. But close your eyes now and think about it. When you are ready, open your eyes. Without blinking or closing your eyes, instantly recall and feel the experience and when you have done so, say, yes.

• • • • •

Make a list of every possible problem and every possible negative emotion and attitude. Beside each word, include the opposite positive word. For example, hate-love or fear-courage, etc. When upset, look over the list, think about the dirty tricks you play on yourself and others psychologically, then pray and try some of the above ideas.

Prayer and divine healing are a reality according to Dr. Randy Byrd, M.D. who conducted a double-blind study of 400 cardiovascular patients reported in *Medical News*, March 3, 1986. Unbeknown to the patients or their treating physicians, half of the patients were prayed for and half weren't. In the group not prayed for, 16 required antibiotics, 18 suffered pulmonary edema and 12 required insertion of a breathing tube into the trachea, compared to the prayed-for group among which only 3 required antibiotics, only 6 suffered pulmonary edema and none required intubation. This double-blind controlled scientific study offers validation that God will intervene on our behalf when we pray to Him. Amen.

• • • • •

When you are ready, complete the affirmations below.

I, _____ YOUR NAME _____ , forgive myself and _____ NAMES OF OTHERS _____ and release them into the hands of God.

I, _____ YOUR NAME _____ , release every problem to God as Lord of my life for His analysis, solution and disposition.

I, _____ YOUR NAME _____ , express my personal power only with love and compassion to glorify God with my heart and my life.

• • • • •

Now that I know who I am, a little child in Your big hands, dear God, I open up my heart, my life and my eyes and I see Your love and eternity and I am with You to the end of all time. But when I stumble and fall and get stuck in this world, again and again, I only see poor little me and no end in sight for my hurting and worry. And when I have had enough of my sorrow and the sooner the better, I thank You, God, for helping me open my eyes to see You and me together again forever.

HEALING STEP 2: Nurture, Cleanse, Heal Whole Person

True holistic health is a state of unity with God, allowing His will to flow unobstructed through His creation, your body, mind and spirit. Disease is separation from God, rebelling against His will and His authority in your life.

Healing for the whole person is your natural reward for prayer, affirmations, meditation, submitting to God, walking with God, inviting His living Holy Spirit into your heart, blessing your body with only healthful foods, correcting underlying metabolic disturbances, detoxifying and cleansing your body, strengthening your immune system and exercise.

A comprehensive health program is necessary to successfully treat any health problem in the short and long run, although it may take longer and be more complex than the typical quick fix orthodox piecemeal treatment which produces only partial success in treating health problems.

In that over 90% of all of our physical, emotional and mental health problems are caused by the food we eat, the Detox Diet of good, wholesome, nutritious food is recommended as a permanent diet to keep you healthy, fit and slim.

The Detox Diet cleanses and detoxifies the body in addition to providing the nutrients it needs to maintain and rejuvenate itself. The Detox Diet is a way of fasting every day and fasting and resting the body is the most natural way to detoxify and heal the body. The Detox Diet of grains, vegetables and fruit, detoxifies and neutralizes the acidic toxins from unhealthful foods, smoking, alcohol, coffee, medical and street drugs, etc.

TEMPORARY ALKALINE DIET

Essentially, systemic toxicity is an acidic condition which can be corrected over a period of time by the Detox Diet, by eliminating bad habits and by correcting underlying metabolic imbalances and diseases. For immediate relief from the above symptoms, eat a temporary diet of only alkaline cooked vegetables for 1 to 3 days to de-acidify and detoxify the body in a controlled and efficient manner. The temporary alkaline diet is recommended before and after fasting and during any illness and when you are feeling better, return to the Detox Diet of grains, vegetables, fruit, lentils, fish and eggs.

The emergency alkaline diet detoxifies and de-acidifies the acids, toxins, wastes, poisons from too much meat, dairy products, free oils, junk foods, chemicalized foods, cigarettes, alcohol, coffee, street drugs, medical drugs, hypothyroidism, candidiasis, chronic Epstein-Barr virus, food allergy, etc. which create general toxicity in all cells and tissues of the body, including the lymph system and bloodstream, causing acidity, inflammation, congestion, infection, swelling, edema, nerve irritation, tight muscles, pain, constipation, neck, back and spinal problems, arthritis, cardiovascular disease, cancer and practically any other illness or disease. Systemic toxicity, in fact, is the basic cause of all disease as outlined by Dr. Henry Bieler, M.D. in *Food Is Your Best Medicine* and Dr. John Tilden, M.D., in *Toxemia Explained.*

The alkaline diet consists of cooked root and green leafy vegetables. Not included are any seeds, seed tops, florets or seeds (do not eat broccoli, cauliflower, asparagus, for example), beans lentils or nuts which are concentrated amino acid proteins which can cause acidity or allergic reactions to the proteins found in them.

The alkaline diet, also known as the potato diet, includes only certain steamed, boiled or baked vegetables and they are: potatoes, sweet potatoes, yams, squash, pumpkin, carrots, beets, jicama, all greens, cabbage, parsley and celery — all cooked. Also recommended is 2 to 3 quarts of filtered or distilled water and also herb tea. Restrict seasoning to sea salt and mild herbs and limit their use.

In between meals, eat peeled apples, apple sauce, apple juice, prunes, prune juice, plums, pears, peaches, nectarines and apricots. No dried fruit. Limit the consumption of fruit to between meals and concentrate mostly on eating the root and leafy vegetables as your mainstay.

If you are allergic to any of the above vegetables, omit them and if allergic to potatoes, substitute red potatoes if tolerated and squash or pumpkin. You should eat some potatoes, squash or pumpkin with breakfast, lunch and dinner along with other vegetables. Do not eat only a couple of vegetables just because it is convenient or because you like them. Go shopping and eat a good variety of the allowable vegetables and fruits.

Make a large pot of alkaline vegetable stew, enough for breakfast, lunch and dinner and supplement it with side dishes of potatoes or steamed greens. Do not add salt or herbs to the vegetable stew during cooking. Omit seasoning altogether and if you have to, add it at the table. This is emphasized because most people have a habit of seasoning everything. Try the vegetables plain for awhile and see how you like them, especially when you are trying to detoxify.

Eat three or more meals a day of the alkaline vegetables. You can usually eat all you want and still lose weight on this temporary diet. Do not skip meals because when you do not eat, your body digests its own toxic muscle protein (amino acids) and toxic stored fats (fatty acids) making you more acidic and toxic.

The alkaline diet is not intended for prolonged use and not recommended for those people who have diarrhea or vomiting lasting more than one day or anyone who has an abnormal alkaline condition as a result of disease. Check with your nutritional medical doctor if you have any questions about the alkaline diet. Orthodox doctors will, no doubt, minimize and criticize this natural therapy.

During the alkaline diet, cleanse your colon with herbal laxatives and colonics or enemas to help eliminate the large amount of stored toxins exiting through the large intestines during the detoxification process.

The alkaline diet was developed by Dr. Steig Erlander, Ph.D., of Altadena, California and is part of his urine pH allergy testing program outlined in the section on allergy. The alkaline diet is used to temporarily alkalize the body. Then eat a suspected allergy food and test the urine with Nitrazine pH testing paper to see if you get an acid allergy reaction to that particular food. It is very accurate, reliable, inexpensive and self-administered.

Before beginning the alkaline diet, test your urine pH and saliva pH with the Nitrazine testing paper, as outlined below.

Since vegetables are high in minerals which help normalize the pH, the temporary alkaline diet is recommended for both acid or alkaline conditions and especially for low pH (acid) of the saliva and urine.

Try the alkaline diet, monitor the saliva and urine pH, cleanse your bowels and watch your health improve. Eat the alkaline diet before and after a fast for a more successful and effective fast.

NOTES ON SALIVA AND URINE ACIDITY OR ALKALINITY

According to the Biological Theory of Ionization put forth

by Dr. Carey Reams, we get life and health from the energy created by the foods we eat. Our bodies are cationic or positively charged and almost all foods are cationic except freshly squeezed lemon juice, which along with a good diet and adequate minerals helps us maintain a proper anion-cation balance necessary for all metabolic functions in the body, especially basic digestion and assimilation of food.

Anion-cation imbalances cause imbalances in the body pH acid-alkaline balance. To test the saliva and urine pH, purchase Nitrazine pH testing paper, which is available without prescription from most pharmacies. Put the end of a small strip of testing paper on your tongue and close your mouth momentarily, remove the testng paper and note any color changes.

Tear off a 2 inch strip of testing paper, sit on the toilet (guys, too), hold one end of the paper strip, urinate on the other end, note the color and compare it to the chart on the package.

If the testing paper remains yellow, your saliva or urine is acid. If the paper turns blue, you are alkaline. The ideal pH of both urine and saliva is 6.40 with a normal range of 6.20 to 6.80, which usually indicates you are on your way to good health. Any pH below 6.20 or above 6.80 can mean a sharp loss in energy and sickness. Your orthodox doctor will tell you that the normal range of both urine and saliva pH is 4.50 to 7.50 in an effort to dissuade you. Find a nutritionally oriented doctor who will support your efforts.

The best times to check the pH is 11 a.m. and 2 p.m.

In some people, the pH may be a little more acid or lower in the morning as a result of digesting our own acidic fat and protein stores in our bodies during the night. Any deviation, higher or lower than pH 6.40 during the day, can indicate a loss of energy and sickness. Your alternative doctor can help you learn how to achieve the proper anion-cation balance.

When the pH of your saliva or urine is not 6.40 or below the normal range of 6.20 or above 6.80 most of the time or when your pH changes below or above the normal range every time you eat, this can mean you have a serious mineral deficiency or that you are sick or about to be sick eventually. If both the saliva and urine pH are below 5.40 (very acid) day after day, you need professional help from a nutritional doctor right away.

The pH of a sick person may temporarily read 6.40 but in

all likelihood, the pH will not remain in the normal range for long and it is a good idea to monitor such changes.

The Detox Diet and Wellness Lifestyle is recommended to bring the saliva and urine pH back into the 6.20 and 6.80 normal range. Specifically, a good ionized mineral supplement with marine trace minerals is indicated for all pH deviations to the normal range. Organic chlorine from vegetables, potassium and calcium are especially important. In general, eat more mineral rich vegetables and dextrinized whole grains. A series of colonics is recommended, particularly when the pH is above 7.20. Eat less meat to decrease acidity and, of course, acidic and constipated meat eaters also need colonics.

There are many exceptions to generalizations regarding the proper pH, any deviations and remedial treatment. Hypoglycemics, for example, may not be able to tolerate drinking 2 to 3 quarts of water daily. Therefore, consult a nutritional doctor who specializes in Reams' methods.

For more information on Reams' Biological Theory of Ionization, write to Dr. Joseph Manthei, D.C., 853 Scotland Road, Quarryville, PA 17566, telephone (717) 284-3181. Do not delay and start by ordering the book *Health Through Diet* by Dr. Manthei. It is recommended that all nutritional chiropractors order the home study course in BTI offered by Dr. Manthei.

FASTING

Fasting is a method of resting, cleansing, detoxifying and healing the body to stop the insidious degeneration of our cells, tissues, bones, organs, glands, nerves and brain caused by accumulated toxins from unhealthful foods and bad habits. The body degenerates in a poisoned state of toxicity and it heals only when it is clean, unobstructed and nurtured with organic, chemical-free, living enzymes, vitamins, minerals, amino acids, fatty acids, carbohydrates, fiber and other nutrients from fresh, living foods.

Fasting, along with a complete detoxification program, will promote healing of old injuries from accidents. Men and women disabled with back problems can heal and go back to work. Fasting can clear up chronic gastrointestinal gas and constipation. Fasting makes you feel peaceful and meditative. Put fasting to work for you.

Many people — even health oriented individuals — are

unaware of being toxic. They make the mistake of beginning a fast only on water or fruit juice which causes a too rapid detox-ification process of too many accumulated toxins in cells and tissues being dumped into the lymph and bloodstream too quickly. The exiting and free circulating poisons then overwhelm the eliminative organs causing an out of control healing crisis, acidity, nausea, headache, weakness, dizziness, irritability, depression, hunger attacks, allergy-addiction withdrawal symptoms, colds, sinus problems, achiness, pain, skin eruptions and exacerbation of old health problems.

Not a very pleasant fast. No wonder that you have to break the fast prematurely and start eating again just to get rid of the above cleansing crisis and withdrawal symptoms.

For a more comfortable and successful fast, neutralize most of the acid toxins first by eating the alkaline diet for 1 to 3 days, then fast for 1 to 3 days and break the fast with the alkaline diet for another 1 to 3 days or at least with one or two meals of alkaline vegetables.

You will detoxify just as quickly but with far fewer reactions and symptoms of toxic release. Your immune system may be able to keep you on top of any unnecessary infection from the releasing poisons. You may still have a healing crisis with its associated symptoms but it should be more mild and should not devastate you.

It is very important to eliminate the escaping toxins by cleaning out your bowels daily during fasting and the detoxification program by taking both an herbal laxative and a colonic or enema. In addition, drink sarsparilla tea upon rising and at bedtime to help bind and eliminate the intestinal toxins. And take 1 to 2 tablespoons activated charcoal stirred in water in between meals and before bed and drink 2 glasses of water each time to absorb and eliminate the intestinal toxins.

Also take a bulk intestinal cleanser like psyllium seed husks only if it helps speed elimination. If your intestines are too obstructed or unhealthy, a bulk fiber product may constipate you more. It could help you later but maybe not now. Note that some people may become allergic to psyllium as a result of taking it too long, causing hayfever, sinus problems, sore throat, gastrointestinal upset, etc. You can test for allergy to it with the urine pH allergy testing program. A good guide to prevent an allergy to psyllium is to take it for 4 weeks and then switch to something else and then you can return to it again if necessary. After eating the alkaline diet for 1 to 3 days, begin the fast with 2 to 3 quarts of filtered or distilled water, hot herb tea, fresh carrot juice, carrot juice mixed with beet, beet tops, parsley, celery, Romaine lettuce, spinach or any other mild greens. When possible and affordable, drink up to 2 quarts of fresh vegetable juice a day along with another quart of filtered or distilled water. Drink 2 quarts (64 oz.) of the vegetable juice undiluted by drinking 8 oz. every 2 hours. Or if weak or very ill, dilute the vegetable juice about 30% by adding 2 cups (16 oz.) pure water to 2 quarts of fresh vegetable juice making a total of 80 oz. and drink 10 oz. diluted vegetable juice every 2 hours.

This will be enough nourishment for 16 waking hours. If you wake up in the night hungry, drink more vegetable juice. Put these fresh juices in your health program budget. They are worth the expense ounce for ounce!!!

While fasting, whole fruit is recommended over fruit juice. A general rule is to avoid fruit juice because too much is usually taken and it can cause blood sugar imbalances, too many emotional highs, hyperactivity, temper tantrums and emotional upsets followed inevitably by emotional lows, depression and self-destructive behavior.

Now some people can handle fruit juice and fruit smoothies which are wonderful but a lot of people cannot. If you do drink fruit juices on a fast, limit the quantity, eat some whole fruit instead and drink mostly vegetable juices which balance your energy better than fruit juice or whole fruit.

Eat whole fresh fruit separately from drinking the vegetable juices to avoid indigestion. The best fruits for cleansing and fasting are the juicy fruits papaya, pineapple, cherries, orange, tangerine, grapefruit, melon (eat alone), juicy not dry pears, juicy sweet not dry sour apples, etc. Grapes are not included because many people who are toxic get reactions, indigestion and cramps from eating grapes, especially on an empty stomach or during emotional upset. Bananas and other less juicy fruits are OK but concentrate more on eating the more juicy fruits.

Eat a limited amount of whole fruit in between drinking the vegetable juices, say some fruit once in the morning and maybe two times in the afternoon. For those of you with sensitive sleeping patterns, stop eating all fruit or drinking fruit juice after 3 p.m.

to avoid insomnia or sleep disturbances. Instead, drink vegetable juice in the evenings or if you wake up hungry.

If drinking vegetable juice and eating whole fruit according to the above schedule is not ''satisfying'' your appetite or energy needs, be patient because your toxic body with its over stimulated and worn-out adrenals, edgy nervous system, allergies, addictions and withdrawal symptoms will settle down after a day or so and you will feel more grounded and peaceful.

However, to help you get through the rough part of the fast, drink warm herbal tea (red clover blossom, ginger, linden flower, licorice, blackberry, raspberry, chamomile, hibiscus, etc.) with no caffeine. Drinking warm herbal tea right before you drink the vegetable juice or eat the fruit relaxes your gastrointestinal tract, makes you feel better and helps you stay on your fast. Drinking warm plain pure water beforehand helps, too. If very ''hungry,'' drink warm alkaline vegetable broth before drinking the vegetable juice. Of course, do not mix vegetable broth with fruit.

If the fast becomes unbearable, eat a good meal of cooked alkaline vegetables, clean out your colon with an herbal laxative and an enema or colonic, rest and then continue the fast.

If all of this doesn't work, it may mean you are terribly toxic or having some powerful withdrawal symptoms from allergy-addiction to unhealthful foods or bad habits. Or it may mean that you are fighting yourself by pretending to be undisciplined to give you an excuse to stop the fast. If you cannot get past your resistance in this regard, stop the fast and try again when you make up your mind to take positive action instead of doing everything possible to sabotage your fast and health program.

Break the fast by eating the cooked alkaline vegetables for 1 to 3 days or at least eat one or two meals of the alkaline vegetables. Then eat the foods in the cleansing diet keeping it on the bland side at first until your body can handle solid food again.

As outlined in the chapter on Weight Loss, prolonged fasting and weight loss dieting have some serious medical risks and should be supervised by an alternative medical doctor.

Read *How to Keep Slim, Healthy and Young with Juice Fasting* by Dr. Paavo Airola, Ph.D., N.D., *Fasting Can Save Your Life* by Dr. Herbert Shelton, *Colon Health* by Dr. Norman Walker, Ph.D., and *Charcoal Startling New Facts About the World's Most Powerful Clinical Adsorbent* by Drs. Agatha and Calvin Thrash, M.D.

COLONICS

Cleanse your colon regularly with the cleansing diet, eliminate the poisons and toxicity created by underlying metabolic disorders, give up unhealthful foods and bad habits which pollute the colon and the whole body, fast periodically, exercise to move those toxins out and take herbal laxatives, enemas and colonics to clean up what no other therapy can as quickly and efficiently.

One colonic per day is recommended by alternative doctors for 7 days, then one per week or an extra one if you become ill, overly fatigued, depressed, irritable, gassy, etc. and repeat the 7 day colonic program every 6 weeks as long as necessary. See the section on colonics for a list of supplements and things to do when taking colonics.

Why 7 or more colonics consecutively? The first colonic cleans the colon a little and each succeeding colonic irrigation cleans more and more out higher and higher into the colon. Cleansing herbs, vitamin C, acidolphilus and bulk fiber greatly aid the process of deep cleansing and healing.

Then one colonic per week helps keep you clean and honest. Your tummy will flatten and feel light, you will have less gas and discomfort. You will feel better. If you cheat with unhealthful foods and bad habits, you will be clean and sensitive enough to know it because your colon will immediately speak to you, saying, ''Stop stuffing, bloating, poisoning, gassing and killing me or you'll be sorry because I will make you pay.'' Once you get to that stage where your body and colon are clean, you will not get away with cheating and you may not want to cheat at all or not nearly as often.

SUPPLEMENTS: HERBS, ENZYMES AND GLANDULARS

A good detoxification program should include supplements, herbs, enzymes, glandulars and other food grade nutrients to help detoxify, stimulate and rebuild the eliminative organs and the immune system.

Liver: Detoxifying and regenerating the liver is of primary importance. In addition to treating the liver directly, the cleansing diet and a series of colonics will significantly cleanse the colon and reduce the amount of intestinal bacteria, fecal matter, toxins, immune complexes and other antigenic material absorbed through the intestinal walls into the portal blood circulation to the liver for detoxification.

Eating properly and cleansing the colon as well as correcting candidiasis, hypothyroidism, sources of free radical pathology and other underlying metabolic disturbances will build up the immune system of the colon wall and help keep the intestinal toxins in the colon where they belong, help prevent them from passing through the colon wall and into the bloodstream and therefore help limit or stop the toxins from overloading the liver which detoxifies these colon toxins.

Detoxification of the colon and building up the immune system of the colon wall is therefore the first step in improving the liver functions of filtering toxins from the bloodstream, neutralizing these toxins, production of metabolic enzymes, production of bile necessary for digestion and assimilation, phagocytosis (engulfing and neutralizing foreign substances) and elimination of immune complexes and other antigenic allergy material. In short, the liver will function more efficiently to filter and eliminate toxins from the blood when the colon is clean and not sending unnecessary large amounts of toxins to the liver for detoxification.

Send a lot of love, not grief, to your liver, stop poisoning it nonchalantly and casually demanding that it detoxify all the chemicals, street drugs, medical drugs, alcohol, cigarettes, dietary toxins, coffee, dairy, free oils, food allergens, heavy metals, industrial fumes, free radicals, germs, candida and colon toxins. Your liver is pleading, ''Give me a break. Don't you like me?''

Of course you like your liver and prove it by giving it the following natural therapies to stimulate bile production and flow, to protect it from inflammatory and free radical damage, to help it regenerate and to help it phagocytize bacteria, antigen-antibody complexes and other toxins by stimulating its Kupffer cells.

Treat the liver three times daily with meals with silymarin from milk thistle seed extract 150 mg three times and dandelion root 4 g or extract 250 - 500 mg each three times and vitamin C 2 g two or three times.

Drink 16 oz. room temperature pure water with the juice of one lemon upon rising and if your doctor permits, repeat the lemon water mid-morning, mid-afternoon and mid-evening in between meals or snacks.

Spleen: The spleen and the lymph system are also important in detoxification. The spleen is part of the lymph system and the function of the spleen in detoxifying the blood is similar to the lymph nodes detoxifying the lymph fluid.

The macrophages of the spleen cleanse the blood by phagocytizing (engulfing and digesting) unwanted debris, bacteria, pus, parasites, old and abnormal red blood cells and abnormal platelets. The lymphocytes of the spleen are involved along with the bone marrow, thymus and liver in forming antibodies and sensitized lymphocytes to attack and destroy invading organisms, foreign bodies and toxins.

Treat the spleen to enhance splenic blood flow, macrophage and lymphocyte activity by taking three times daily with meals barberry root 1 - 2 g three times, desiccated spleen 350 mg three times and continue taking the vitamin C, dandelion and goldenseal previously recommended for liver problems which will also help the function of the spleen.

Lymphatic System: Toxic lymph is just as important as the concept of toxic blood and both the lymph and the blood need to be cleaned up as part of the detoxification treatment program. The clear liquid in interstitial tissues and lymph vessels is called lymph and in the blood, it is called plasma. The lymph carries nutrients from the arterial capillaries to the nearby cells and then carries the cell wastes to the venous capillaries. About nine-tenths of the lymph is reabsorbed through the venous blood capillaries and the remaining one-tenth of lymph fluid is reabsorbed through lymphatic capillaries, especially the larger protein and particulate matter too large to be reabsorbed by the venous capillaries.

All tissues of the body with the exception of a few have lymphatic channels that drain excess fluid directly from the interstitial spaces between cells in the body tissues, lymph nodes, tonsils, adenoids, liver, spleen, thymus and intestines. The macrophages in the lymph tissue ingest foreign material, bacteria and toxins and the lymphocytes, as in the spleen, are important in antibody formation and immunological reactions.

The lymphatic system is also one of the major routes for absorption of nutrients from the gastrointestinal tract, especially fats. Therefore, it is easy to see that eating toxic fats filled with poisons and free radicals poisons the lymph system. About half the lymph is formed in the intestines and liver and this is why it is so important to keep the intestines and liver as clean as possible with diet and bowel cleansing.

Toxins accumulate in the lymph lymph vessels and lymph nodes causing congestion, stasis, inflammation, infection, swelling, edema, pain, cancer, etc. Lymphatic flow and macrophage and lymphocyte functions can be improved with vitamin C 2,000 mg three times daily, glycyrrhiza from licorice root 1 g three times daily and echinacea root 400 mg three times daily (use echinacea for no longer than two weeks and not all the time to avoid depressing the immune system), vitamin A in small doses for only two weeks to avoid toxicity. Carotene, zinc and astragalus to be discussed below with the immune system.

Most important: Vitamins C and A.

Lymphatic flow can also be stimulated by exercise, stretching, elevation of extremities, postural inversion on a slant board, massage, especially lymphatic massage and hot and cold baths.

Kidneys: The kidneys are important eliminative organs and are often abused and damaged by toxic protein acids from an inability to digest proteins, excess salt, coffee, alcohol, dairy, free oils, fats, sugar, aspirin, pain killers, diuretics, birth control pills, other medications, street drugs, mercury and chemicals in foods and the workplace.

After many years of abuse, the kidneys become worn out from filtering and eliminating these unnecessary poisons from the blood. As a compensation due to excess toxicity, the adrenals are stimulated somewhat akin to whipping a dead horse to secrete large amounts of adrenoxidase to help oxidize the poisons in the kidneys. Over a period of years, the kidneys as well as the adrenal glands and the heart are worn out from increasing toxicity and high blood pressure.

Excess poisons in the blood which the kidneys and other overloaded eliminative organs are unable to remove are deposited and accumulated in the body cells and tissues causing systemic toxicity or the poisons exit through vicarious or alternate eliminative pathways of the prostate, breast and uterus causing cancer or other degenerative problems.

Kidney and adrenal dysfunction causes fatigue, swelling, puffiness and edema around the eyes, face and body, blurred vision, high blood pressure, nausea, bad taste in mouth, frequent urination, recurring kidney/bladder infections, kidney stones and, lest we forget, uremic poisoning and congestive heart failure, the fourth leading cause of death in the United States.

The best way to help worn-out kidneys is give them a rest by fasting, eliminate acids from meat by eliminating it from the diet, add fish and eggs when better, and drink 2 to 3 quarts of pure water daily.

For kidney infection, take the supplements and herbs recommended below under immune system.

For acute kidney stone obstruction, take the herb ammi visnaga 1 oz. made into a tea every 3 hrs. and rubia tinctura, rumex crispus or aloe vera at below laxative doses. Also apply hot fomentation wrapped around the kidney — place in back and around the abdomen.

When the stones are calcium oxalate, acidify the urine with ascorbic acid with no sugar. Avoid oxalic acid foods, spinach, cranberry, chard, beet tops, chocolate and tea, black or green. Eliminate dairy. Daily take vitamin B6 25 mg and vitamin K 2 mg to help control production of oxalic acid and magnesium 600 mg to increase the solubility of calcium oxalate and inhibit its precipitation and deposition. Take the herbs rubia tinctura, rumex crispus or aloe vera in a dose below the laxative effect.

For uric acid stones, alkalize the urine with citrate, bicarbonate and the alkaline diet. Eliminate all purines found in meat, fish, poultry and yeast. Add fish later when better. Daily take folic acid 5 mg to promote purine scavenging and xanthine oxidate inhibition.

For cystine stones, alkalize the urine and avoid methionine-rich foods, dairy, soy, wheat, meats, fish, lima beans, garbanzo beans, mushrooms and all nuts except coconut, hazelnut and sunflower seeds.

For magnesium ammonium phosphate stones, acidify the urine.

Blood: To purify toxic blood, take 1 cup of tea 2 to 8 times a day pau d'arco or taheebo, red clover blossom and sarsaparilla. Recall that sarsaparilla tea binds bacterial toxins in the intestines keeping them out of the bloodstream. Eat fresh blueberries 4 oz. three times a day to decrease the permeability of the blood-brain barrier against drugs, pollutants and toxins linked to cerebral allergies, schizophrenia and auto-immune diseases of the central nervous system. Also take L-carnitine 500 mg to 1 g three times a day to lower blood ammonia levels.

Gastrointestinal Tract: Digestion, assimilation and elimination are improved by eating the Detox Diet and cleansing the colon with herbal laxatives and a series of colonics. The most effective aid to digestion, if you need it, is plant enzymes with lipase, amylase, protease, cellulase enzymes and some brands include acidolphilus also. Take daily.

Some people may require supplementation with hydrochloric acid tablets and pancreatic enzymes, which may cause gastrointestinal distress for around two weeks when you first start taking them. Low hydrochloric acid can cause indigestion and poor assimilation; in addition, inadequate hydrochloric acid can cause allergy, infection and candidiasis and hydrochloric acid tablets are a treatment for these conditions. Note that low hydrochloric acid output may be caused by hiatal hernia interference with the vagus nerve supply to the stomach and its ability to manufacture hydrochloric acid.

Generally, it is best to take the plant enzymes and pancreatic enzymes at the beginning of the meal and then take hydrochloric acid after the meal to aid digestion, if necessary. This sequence will give the pancreatic enzymes a better chance of maximum activity in a more alkaline environment. One of the reasons why plant enzymes are superior is that they are more stable and reach peak activity in either an alkaline or acid medium.

A Comprehensive Stool and Digestive Analysis (see Toxicity chapter) is recommended to test how you are digesting and assimilating your food and this test will give you information on just about everything you need to know about your health.

Acidolphilus, the friendly bacteria, decreases the activity of carcinogenic organisms and synthesizes the antimicrobal substances lactic acid, acetic acid, benzoic acid and hydrogen peroxide, acidolin, acidophilin, lactocidin which inhibit the growth and toxin production of various, potentially dangerous, dietary pathogens. Acidolphilus inhibits E. coli bacteria responsible for traveler's diarrhea; therefore, you would want to take acidolphilus before, during and after trips to other states or foreign countries. Acidolphilus also inhibits urinary tract infections, herpes and candidi. The most effective strains of acidolphilus are NCFM, N2 and ADH and should be stored in air-tight, dark refrigerated containers.

General Metabolic: The term ''essential'' oils means just that. Essential linolenic and linoleic oils and fatty acids are ''essential'' and "necessary" for life meaning that if you do not include linolenic and linoleic oils in your diet on a daily basis, you cannot enjoy life, healthwise, to the fullest. Read the chapter on Oils and Fats.

Essential oils are required in every metabolic process in YOUR body and if you don't include them in your diet on a routine basis, just watch your hair fall out, skin erupt and dry up like a prune, liver degenerate, behavior deteriorate, kidneys act up, glands shrivel, infections repeat and repeat, wound healing slow down, become sterile, wife miscarry her baby, lose your vision, learn and remember less and less, get weak, and develop arthritis, cancer, cardiovascular disease and other degenerative diseases.

Your diet of polyunsaturated vegetable oils, (including olive oil), margarine, mayonnaise, butter, lard, beef fat, etc. won't save you either because they contain non-essential fatty acids and very little, if any, essential linolenic and linoleic oils. If you are on some type of ill-advised oil and fat restricted weight or "health" program or if you do not include at least 10% of your calories in essential oils daily, it is like putting a gun to your head and slowly pulling the trigger finally blowing out what is left of your brains; it all catches up with you around middle age when you start falling apart and developing cancer, cardiovascular disease, or arthritis just like half the population as the result of not eating essential oils.

To avoid middle age collapse, eat fresh, clean fish outlined in the chapter on meat, fish and eggs; take omega-3 and omega-6 rich fish oil and borage oil combination capsules; and freshly ground and/or creamed in water flax, pumpkin, sunflower, sesame seeds daily which are the most important sources of essential linolenic and linoleic fatty acids.

Immune System: Alternative natural therapies correct the causes of a depressed immune system and orthodox medicine only treats the symptoms with antibiotics and other medications. The missing link in the germ theory of disease in Establishment medicine is potentiating or activating the immune system to build your resistance to the ever present germs. Germs are everywhere present in your body and in the environment and that includes the polio virus, staph, E. coli, candida, etc. The reason you do not get a disease from these germs is because your resistance is high enough to fight them off.

Nutritionally oriented medical doctors, chiropractors and naturopaths build up your resistance and immunity to bacteria, viruses, yeast germs, fungus, parasites and worms by:

(1) reducing stress with spiritual and lifestyle counseling to decrease stress-induced increases in corticosteroids, catecholamines and cyclic AMP which lead to immuno-suppressed state leaving the host susceptible to infections and such degenerative diseases as cancer, arthritis, cardiovascular disease and others;

(2) identifying and correcting any underlying metabolic disorders which are the primary and original cause of immuno-suppression, namely, hypothyroidism, candidiasis, chronic Epstein-Barr virus, food allergy, hypoglycemia, systemic toxicity, free radical pathology or other metabolic imbalances;

(3) recommending the cleansing diet and cleansing the colon to strengthen the immune system of the colon wall to prevent toxins, germs and other organisms from passing through the colon wall into the bloodstream, lymphatics and abdominal cavity and from there into the whole body;

(4) administration of desiccated thymus gland extract to build up the immune system; take at least 300 mg or up to 10 tablets once or twice a day for 3 to 6 weeks; note that thymus gland therapy is often effective with stubborn staph infections when taken in large dosage for 6 weeks or longer;

(5) adequate protein is essential for optimal immune function and the liver, for example, will not heal properly unless a good source of protein is eaten; eat ocean fish with scales and fins and organically raised eggs twice a week; organic beef and chicken are also acceptable;

(6) eliminate all sugars to fight infection; table sugar, fructose, honey, maple syrup, brown rice syrup, barley malt syrup and fruits all significantly reduce neutrophil phagocytosis and depress lymphocyte activity; when the infection is over, limit use of honey, maple syrup, brown rice syrup and barley malt syrup;

(7) lose weight because obesity is associated with decreased immune status as well as atherosclerosis, hypertension, diabetes mellitus and joint disorders;

(8) eliminate free oils and toxic fats which increase levels of cholesterol, free fatty acids, triglycerides and bile acids causing inhibition of various immune functions, including lymphocyte activity, response to mitogens, antibody response, PMN chemotaxis and phagocytosis as well as causing free radical pathology;

(9) eliminating alcohol which increase the susceptibility to infections in animals and profound depression of lymphocytes in humans; alcoholics are known to be more susceptible to pneumonia;

(10) drinking lots of pure water, full strength or diluted vegetable juices, alkaline vegetable broth and herb teas; 2 to 3 quarts a day are recommended to flush out the system;

(11) correcting vitamin, mineral and amino acid deficiencies associated with lowered resistance to infection, specifically vitamins A, B-complex, B6, beta-carotene, C, E, folic acid, iron, zinc, manganese and trace minerals;

(12) recommending the following supplements and herbs: take vitamin C 500 mg every two hours; bioflavonoids 1 g daily; vitamin A 50,000 IU for no longer than two weeks to avoid toxicity (some people can tolerate up to 200,000 IU vitamin A for up to two weeks but this can only be done under medical supervision) or beta-carotene 200,000 IU daily (in hypothyroidism take vitamin A because hypothyroids may not be able to assimilate beta-carotene); zinc 30 mg daily; thymus extract 300 mg or up to 10 tablets twice a day as indicated above; echinacea root 1-2 g three times daily; goldenseal root 1-2 g three times daily; poke plant root 500 mg three times daily; astragalus root 5-15 g three times a day and acidolphilus three times daily.

In addition, for a cold or flu or an active stubborn infection of germs, virus or parasites anywhere in the body, take the following natural antibiotics twice daily upon rising and at bedtime: 2 to 4 oz. Dr. Donsbach's Super Oxy hydrogen peroxide premixed in aloe juice along with 2 tablets catalase and other antioxidant enzymes to neutralize any free radicals from the hydrogen peroxide; also try Dr. Donsbach's nasal spray and ear drops with diluted hydrogen peroxide; 10 drops Aerox or Aerobic 07 stabilized oxygen in 8 oz. water; also brush your teeth with 20 drops of Aerox or Aerobic 07 mixed in a little water; also gargle with diluted Aerobic 07; 2 drops of grapefruit seed extract oil mixed in citrus juice; and be sure to take the vitamin A as indicated above, especially in the form of liquid mycelized vitamin A which is assimilated more easily. Most people feel relief from infection in eight hours.

Note that common sources and causes of germ, virus and parasite infection are tap water, dirty water purification systems, leftovers, dried fruit, seafood, raw fish, raw fruits and vegetables (soak and wash with hydrogen peroxide or stabilized oxygen).

CHIROPRACTIC-HOLISTIC

A holistic chiropractor treats the whole person, body, mind and spirit, with spiritual counseling, nutritional counseling, detox-ification, massage and other bodywork and chiropractic adjustments of the spine and other joints in the body.

Holistic chiropractors promote the holistic approach to avoid the non-existent separation of body, mind and spirit. Doctors of chiropractic learned in chiropractic college that God created man, that His universal love and life force directs man especially by way of his brain and spinal nerves to all parts of his body, and that every individual cell has an inborn divine intelligence and ability to heal itself.

It is recommended that all chiropractors treat the body, mind and spirit holistically; warm up the patient with massage, bodywork and hot packs first before making spinal adjustments; provide nutritional counseling; advise to sleep on back or sides (not abdomen) with arms lower than shoulders; help patients treat underlying metabolic disorders; encourage patients to eliminate unhealthful foods and habits; and give the patient what he really needs — faith, hope and belief in himself and God.

A good deep massage and bodywork can make you feel great and if you try to improve your spiritual life, diet, habits and metabolic problems at the same time, you will continue to feel great and you will get better all the time.

If stress from a bad relationship with God, bad foods, bad habits, bad attitudes and a bad work environment are getting you down, try massage once a week at least. Good bodywork is not the answer to everything but often it can wake up, relax and provide relief for those who are stressed out.

Chiropractic adjustments mobilize spinal and joint fixations to improve and normalize the blood and nerve supply to a sick body, a sick mind or a sick spirit. The body then begins to heal itself but with limitations until spiritual and personal alienation, unhealthful foods, bad habits and underlying metabolic disorders are corrected.

The spinal adjustments and bodywork may at times make the person feel worse temporarily because mobilizing the spine and massaging the body of a toxic person can be like stirring up a hornet's nest.

Spinal adjustments and bodywork do loosen up accumulated toxins and poisons which are dumped from toxic tissues into the bloodstream and lymph where they irritate, overstimulate and exacerbate pre-existing inflammations, congestion, muscle tightness and degenerative conditions heretofore either ignored or improperly diagnosed and treated.

Toxic, sick patients need both spinal manipulation and a complete detox and health program to help the adjustment hold, to keep the spine moving freely and to help the body continue to heal itself.

This is both the promise and the threat of holistic chiropractic doctors. The promise of getting well and the threat of having to give up an unhealthful lifestyle. The new you waits for the old you to let go and let God.

Refer to end of the book to order Dr. Deal's paper on Chiropractic Protocol for details on holistic chiropractic examination and treatment.

EXERCISE

Exercise regularly to improve cardiovascular and lymphatic circulation, tone muscles, build strong bones (and prevent osteoporosis), lose weight and raise the spirit. Yoga, stretching, aerobics, tai chi, martial arts, aquacise, fast walking, hiking and swimming will make you feel and look better.

Bouncing on a trampoline is excellent for stimulating and cleansing the lymphatic system and general circulation.

Avoid exercises which traumatize the joints or muscles. Many cannot tolerate the stress to joints caused by running. Go slowly to build up your tolerance, flexibility and strength.

HEALING STEP 3: Wellness and Repeat Treatment

Repeat treatment may be needed in some cases every four to six months. Fasting, colonics, detoxification, weight loss, immune system stimulation and treatment of candidiasis, toxicity, allergy, hypoglycemia and other underlying metabolic disorders may be necessary on a routine basis every four to six months for the rest of your life.

It took you many years of poor health habits to make you unhealthy and susceptible to illness and it may take repeated treatments to repair your health.

Candidiasis, for example, tends to recur despite a good health program and you may need to treat it once or twice a year indefinitely. The most common mistake is to forget about candidiasis and say, ''Oh, I used to have candidiasis years ago.'' Well, you might have it again and it could explain why you are having food allergy sensitivity, sinus problems and thousands of candida related illnesses.

If you have a history of hypoglycemia or borderline hypoglycemia, you will always need to watch that you don't eat too many sweets and don't skip too many meals which can make you lightheaded, dizzy and depressed.

If you have hypothyroidism now or in your past, you are likely to need Armour thyroid the rest of your life. If you stopped taking it, you very well may need to take it again and keep taking it.

When was the last time you fasted, did a series of colonics or got a good massage? Like most people, you may tend to let these wonderful therapies slide through your fingers.

If you are feeling a little out of sorts or if you have gotten into real trouble, stiff all over, pain, irritability, depression or been diagnosed with cancer, arthritis, cardiovascular disease, Alzheimer's or some other degenerative disease, wait no more. Find a good alternative doctor and get to work on a good complete health program including resolving the decision to get well, the Detox Diet, the temporary alkaline diet, fasting, cleansing the colon, supplements, chiropractic, massage and exercise.

Spiritual alienation during most of your life will necessitate daily talks and walks with God. It is so easy to fall back into a destructive pattern of hating yourself and God. Obeying the supreme, divine laws of God, prayer, meditation and fellowship with others of a like spirit are important. Spiritual unity with God is step number one in your health program.

HEART ATTACK AND STROKE PREVENTION & TREATMENT

Cardiovascular disease is the number one killer in the United States responsible for the deaths of 1 out of 2 persons. Space restrictions allow only some brief summary notes on this subject. Dosages are not given to encourage you to consult a nutritional doctor to supervise a program of prevention and treatment. Do not discontinue medical drugs unless supervised by your alternative medical doctor, who may gradually decrease the drugs slowly based on your progress using natural therapies.

Free radical pathology, not cholesterol, is the most important cause of cardiovascular disease, cancer and other degenerative diseases. Therefore, decrease free radical damage by eliminating the sources of free radicals, namely, toxic, unhealthful foods, especially dairy, free oils, fats, fried foods, excess meat, alcohol, smoking, street drugs, processed foods and anything making you toxic. Oral and intravenous chelation therapy is recommended to neutralize free radicals. Refer to the chapters on free radical pathology, chelation and oils.

Take fish liver oils or fish liver EPA-DHA concentrate, hawthorne extract concentrate (the flowers and leaves are more potent than berries) and Bio-Therapeutics Vascu-Comp (call 800-553-2370) in strong therapeutic doses supervised by your alternative nutritional doctor to decrease high blood pressure. Take ginkgo extract concentrate to prevent and treat stroke.

HERBS

HERB SEASONING

In a bowl, mix all of the following herbs to make a delicious herb seasoning for general use on sandwiches, salad dressing, vegetables, grains, sauces, etc. Use a food or coffee grinder to grind the herbs.

10 parts Italian mix (oregano, basil, sage, majoram, rosemary, savory and garlic)

10 parts toasted hulled sesame seeds (grind half)

1 part: ground parsley flakes, ground dulse, kelp powder, marjoram, rosemary, sage, thyme, cardamon, coriander, cumin, onion powder, garlic powder, dill weed, paprika

Cayenne pepper to taste

Taste test and keep adding herbs until you like it.

HERB TEAS

Keep a good selection of herbal teas without caffeine available. Take a thermos of hot or cold herbal tea to work as a good substitute for coffee or have hot water and herb teas in convenient bags available for everyone to make their own.

When someone asks, ''What herb teas do you recommend? I never seem to find one I like,'' this usually means they like coffee better and they really don't like herb teas or they think they don't because they have never given them a fair chance and they don't intend to.

Herb tea will not give you a buzz like caffeinated coffee. Personally, I have a natural high most of the time from my good health and natural diet, and other certified health nuts will tell you the same thing and I would rather be a health nut than an unhealthy nut.

Keep on hand one or more of the following herb teas either in bulk or in tea bags. Try different combinations.

Spearmint, peppermint, wintergreen, chamomile, licorice, fennel, sassafras, lemongrass, pau d'arco, sarsaparilla, ginger, rosehips, hibiscus, red clover blossom, stevia (sweetener), Select (brand name) sweet cherry and vanilla, San Francisco Herb triple berry, Celestial Seasonings blackberry, raspberry, cranberry or apple spice, Stash wintermint, Yogi Tea original or carob mint spice.

HERB TEA: ESSIAC PLUS BIOFLAVONOID FREE RADICAL SCAVENGERS

This herb tea recipe combines the Essiac formula and bioflavonoid free radical scavengers. Drink 8 oz. warm before bed and upon rising or make the lemon-flax shake with this tea instead of water in the morning. The Canadian government sells Essiac tea as a cancer treatment with a medical doctor's prescription. Free radicals attack and damage the genetic structure of the cell causing cancer. Consult a nutritional medical doctor for treatment of cancer.

ESSIAC FORMULA

6½ cups burdock root, cut
16 ounces sheep sorrel herb powder
1 ounce turkey rhubarb root powder
4 ounces slippery elm bark powder

The above measurements represent the proper ratio for ESSIAC tea. The quantity can be reduced to half, for example, simply by reducing the quantity of each herb to half to keep the proper ratio.

BIOFLAVONOID HERB ANTIOXIDANT FREE RADICAL SCAVENGERS

Equal parts: milk thistle seed, elderberry, oregon grape root, white oak bark, hawthorne flowers or leaves (higher than berries), ginkgo leaf.

Mix all of the above, place in a plastic bag and store in refrigerator. To make 2 quarts herb tea, place 1½ cups of the herbs in 2 quarts water in a 5 quart pyrex glass or stainless steel pot. Bring to a boil and reduce heat to a soft rolling boil for 10 minutes. Cover and cool slowly for six hours. Stir periodically. Let it sit for another two hours. Bring to a boil again. Cool it down and while still very warm, strain first in a collander and then a strainer. Place in a 2 quart storage jar and add enough water to make 2 quarts. The storage jar should be dark in color to prevent light from spoiling the tea or place in a clear jar and put the jar in an opaque bag.

Store in refrigerator. Heat 4 oz. distilled water to a boil and add to 8 oz. tea., stir and drink warm before bed and upon rising.

Tea can be added to a lemon-flax shake. Place 8 oz. tea in a blender with 1 oz. freshly ground flax seed, 1 oz. freshly ground milk thistle seed, 2 g vitamin C, 4 ice cubes and blend until smooth. Add juice of freshly squeezed lemon. Drink upon rising on an empty stomach. Milk thistle detoxifies the liver and flax is a treatment for cancer.

Some may prefer to drink the warm tea before bed and then drink the lemon-flax shake upon rising.

HIATAL HERNIA SYNDROME — IMPORTANT

Do you suffer from problems with digestion, assimilation, elimination, pseudo heart attacks, regurgitation of food, burning sensations under the breastbone, acid indigestion that gets worse when you lie down, inability to breathe deeply, toxicity, organ and gland dysfunction or any other unexplained health problem which seems to get progressively worse?

These symptoms can be caused by hiatal hernia affecting nearly half of all adults. Why is this condition so common? Obesity, obesity during pregnancy, nutritional deficiencies, widespread constipation, weak muscles from lack of exercise and perhaps straining at the stool while defecating in the so-called civilized manner sitting on a raised toilet seat instead of properly squatting forces the stomach up abnormally through the weakened (herniated) diaphragm, the breathing muscle, through the opening (hiatus) for the esophagus (food tube).

The upper part of the stomach in this abnormal position squeezes the important vagus nerve which passes through the opening causing vagus nerve interference potentially with every organ and gland enervated and controlled by it. The vagus (vagrant) nerve is everywhere: the medulla, heart, larynx, bronchi, lungs, esophagus, stomach, abdominal blood vessels, liver, gall bladder, pancreas, kidneys, bladder, small intestine, colon and sexual organs — that's just about everything between the base of the brain to the coccyx (tail bone).

"Do you mean possibly that just because I am too fat or that I don't squat to defecate that it causes hundreds of health problems with all those organs and glands in the body?"

Yes, that's exactly what this means!!!

Pressure on the vagus nerve from hiatal hernia interferes with and irritates the vagus throughout the system not just at the point where it is pinched off by the upper part of the stomach. Irritation of the vagus nerve, a parasympathetic nerve, produces acid and lowers the pH within the entire physiological system and upsets the normal acid-alkaline balance in all parts of the body causing dysfunction with all the organs, glands, tissues and cells in the whole body.

The stomach itself is enervated by the vagus nerve which helps control the normal production of hydrochloric acid necessary to properly digest the food you eat and hydrochloric acid concentrations in the blood and tissues also kills germs. As a result of hiatal hernia, interference with the vagus nerve branch to the stomach decreases the production of hydrochloric acid thereby preventing complete digestion and assimilation of nutrients and we literally slowly starve even with the best diet. Low hydrochloric acid increases the potential for infection.

Inability to breathe deeply, one of the major symptoms of hiatal hernia, decreases the amount of oxygen we breathe in and leads to an altered acid condition causing anoxia, acidity, cellular dysfunction, fatigue and degeneration throughout the body.

Vagus nerve. Remember that. Not one of my patients with a medical diagnosis of hiatal hernia ever heard of the vagus nerve or that hiatal hernia causes vagus nerve interference causing a myriad of health problems. All they were told by their Establishment doctor was that they had a condition called hiatal hernia which causes a little indigestion.

A patient with symptoms of indigestion, stomach pain, back pain and acute neck pain with associated dizziness and depression went to a chiropractor after several months of endless medical diagnostic tests and treatment ending up costing over \$20,000. She and her husband were quite upset because her orthodox medical doctor could not find any problems and only gave her antacids and a drug to control excess stomach acid. She went for a second opinion and was told that she was physically healthy and that all her problems were in her head and was referred to a psychiatrist. She knew that she was not crazy and that something physical was wrong with her and that is when she decided to go to a chiropractor because her neck pain was getting worse.

During her initial office visit, the chiropractic doctor did kinesiology and gave her a diagnosis of hiatal hernia and recommended that she lose weight in that she weighed 202 pounds and had two children when she was just about that heavy, all of which can push the stomach up into the chest causing hiatal hernia. She was advised to return to her medical doctor for an x-ray to verify the diagnosis.

After a couple more months delay and during hospitalization for acute problems, her doctors finally gave her an x-ray and found that she did have hiatal hernia because *70% of her stomach was up in her chest.* To my knowledge, her doctors never apologized for telling her that she was crazy or for making her life miserable and they never did offer to return the \$20,000 she paid to them.

Take a look at the following hiatal hernia checklist of symptoms to see what your Establishment doctor may have ''forgotten'' to tell you.

Do you have: belching, bloating, sensitivity at the waist, intestinal gas, regurgitation, hiccups, limited appetite, nausea, vomiting, diarrhea, constipation, colic in children, deep breathing curtailed, fatigue, exhaustion, tendency to swallow air, allergies, dry tickling cough, full feeling at base of throat, pain or burning in upper chest, heartburn, pressure below breastbone, lung pain, rapid heartbeat, rapid rise in blood pressure, pain in left shoulder, left arm or left side of neck, TMJ tempro-mandibular joint pain, bruxism grinding of teeth in sleep, joint pains, localized or overall spinal pain, headaches, dizziness, shakiness, mental confusion, anxiety attacks, insomnia, hyperactivity in children, craving for sugar or alcohol, candidiasis, menstrual difficulties, prostate problems, urinary problems, horseness, obesity and many other symptoms your doctor might like to ignore, minimize and discredit to keep you as a patient longer.

Before allowing your orthodox doctor to cut you open to "explore" or "repair" the hiatal hernia, first try the sensible natural alternatives including, diet, exercise and having a chiropractor, naturopath or nutritional medical doctor pull the stomach down away from the vagus nerve.

Dr. Theodore Baroody, Jr., D.C. in his book *Hiatal Hernia: Insidious Link to Major Illness* recommends the following exercises to benefit patients with hiatal hernia syndrome. Sit in an armchair. Breathe in and hold your breath. Lift both legs up towards the chest. Lower them in steps and exhale. Repeat 3 to 10 times. Another exercise: Drink 16 oz. of warm water and bounce up and down on the heels to help jar the stomach down in place. Patients have reported good results with both exercises when given a chance to help.

Order Dr. Baroody's book by writing to him at 205 Pigeon St., Waynesville, NC 28786 or call him at (704) 456-6231. Mastercard or Visa telephone orders accepted. $10 plus $2.40 postage.

Deep breathing exercises, abdominal exercise and exercise in general will also help.

Since straining at the stool can cause hiatal hernia, assume the squatting position to defecate whenever possible. Replace the standard toilet seat with a soft cushioned seat to make it more comfortable. Purchase from your alternative doctor a special device to raise your knees to your chest.

Also improve chronic constipation by eating high fiber brown rice, buckwheat, millet, raspberries, pears, melon, strawberries, cabbage, asparagus, cucumber, cauliflower, radish, apples, carrots, green peas, beans and lentils.

Improve bowel elimination by taking a series of colonics or enemas along with an herbal laxative. Take one colonic per day for 7 days consecutively, then one per week or when tired or ill and repeat the 7 day cleansing program every 6 weeks for as long as needed.

Avoid antacid tablets which decrease the hydrochloric acid needed to digest your foods. Most antacid medications have aluminum which causes free radical pathology and Alzheimer's or premature senility.

For hiatal hernia syndrome, Dr. D.A. Versendaal, D.C. recommends Standard Process 6 Ligaplex II, 6 Cyruta, 3 CalMa

Plus per day for 3 months. Call Standard Process Lab. 1-800-558-8740 to request the name of the nearest chiropractor or medical doctor who carries these products. Standard Process Lab. is the oldest most respected whole food supplement company in the United States. You may also need to take hydrochloric acid tablets after meals.

Most importantly, consult a chiropractor, naturopath or nutritional medical doctor who knows kinesiology testing for hiatal hernia and can gently pull the stomach down in place with his hands.

With the patient lying on his back with his knees flexed, the doctor uses the pointed fingers of both hands one atop the other to make a contact on the stomach under the ribs and off to the left side to avoid pressure on the aorta. Press the fingers straight in on the stomach to take up the slack and the line of drive is down towards the feet. The patient takes a series of deep breaths. On the in breath, the doctor eases up his contact and on the out breath he goes deep into the abdomen with the line of drive towards the feet. He continues this process for several breaths going deeper and deeper each time and finally gives a harder tug to pull the stomach down out of its trapped position. This procedure should be administered by a chiropractor, naturopath or alternative medical doctor and is contraindicated for ulcers and aortic aneurysm.

This technique should be repeated during each office visit. Some patients get relief with one treatment, others require several treatments and some do not respond at all. Most patients report improvement with specific and overall health problems.

The chiropractic doctor adjusts the vertebrae thoracic 1 through lumbar 5 which provides the nerve supply to all the various organs and glands involved with hiatal hernia syndrome and the vagus nerve. Thoracics 3 to 9 are given special attention to correct spinal problems with the diaphragm, lungs and stomach. Any associated blocks in the cervical spine are also adjusted.

HYPOTHYROIDISM EPIDEMIC IGNORED

Forty percent of all children and adults in America today are suffering needlessly and many are dying unnecessarily from hypothyroidism, one of the underlying metabolic disorders which your orthodox medical doctor routinely misdiagnoses, mistreats, ignores, minimizes and ridicules all in the name of the "science" of modern medicine.

Your Establishment doctor will tell you that the following statements about hypothyroidism are true but they are all false: 1. The blood thyroid tests are the most valid tests available. 2. The basal temperature test is not valid. 3. Synthetic thyroid medication is just as good or better than natural Armour brand thyroid. 4. Iodized salt and the average American diet provide all the necessary iodine and other nutrients your thyroid needs. 5. Hypothyroidism is not an epidemic disease and only quacks represent it as such. 6. Trust your doctor.

Medical testing in general is wrong over half the time and blood thyroid tests measure something other than the presence of thyroid hormone or the thyroid gland's function. Alternative medical doctors across the board recognize the basal temperature test as the best test for hypothyroidism. Synthetic thyroid medication resembles some of the so-called thyroid factors but does not and can not contain all the natural factors in natural thyroid hormone created by God, who is the greatest chemist that no man can ever completely copy despite claims to the contrary. Natural Armour thyroid made from the desiccated thyroid glands of cattle is a food grade medication used with excellent results by all nutritionally oriented medical doctors. Iodized salt and the typical American diet of processed foods provides only one-seventh of the daily requirement for iodine; furthermore, this nutrient depleted diet causes unnecessary degenerative diseases in over half the population. Hypothyroidism is epidemic in this country and a legitimate cause of shame on the medical profession. All of us would like to trust our doctor but unfortunately, he may not deserve our trust.

Too little thyroid hormone in hypothyroidism causes thick, puffy, dry, pale, cool skin and lips, coarse or fine hair, baldness, bluish discoloration of skin, skin problems, eczema, psoriasis, acne, brittle nails, water retention, swelling or edema around the eyes, face, hands, back, ankles, and feet, pot belly or heavy in the upper body, thick tongue, slow speech, hoarseness, impaired memory, muscle weakness or pain, cold sensation, constipation, breathing problems, poor appetite, poor digestion and assimilation, especially calcium and B12, anxiety, depression, insomnia, neuroses, psychoses, slow movements, burning or tingling sensations, palpatations, weak or irregular pulse, pain over heart, weight gain, poor vision, deafness, ear infections, barrenness, infertility, sterility, impotency, low sex drive, prostate problems, irregular, excessive or painful menstruation, ovarian cysts, miscarriage, joint pain, anemia, emotional instability, hyperactivity, poor concentration, irritability, temper tantrums, headaches, migraines, immune dysfunction, frequent infections and a general increase in all metabolic diseases, including arthritis, rheumatoid arthritis, osteoporosis, heart and vascular disease, cancer, lupus, multiple sclerosis, hepatitis, gall bladder disease, kidney disease, etc. The most common complaint is fatigue and waking up tired.

Do you have any of these symptoms? Does your doctor dismiss your complaints as meaningless?

What happens to the patient with fatigue caused by undiagnosed hypothyroidism when he goes to a regular doctor? Most likely, his hypothyroidism is often undetected by blood thyroid tests and remains untreated. The patient continues to complain of fatigue and the doctor continues to give the wrong advice and medication. The patient is referred to a specialist who also ignores the underlying cause and gives the wrong treatment. When the doctor gets tired of hearing the patient complain about fatigue, he will usually refer the patient to a psychiatrist who will usually blame the fatigue and associated depression actually caused by hypothyroidism on some non-existing psychological problem or on a real emotional problem caused by the doctors' own mismanagement of simple hypothyroidism.

A multitude of mental, emotional and behavioral problems are caused by hypothyroidism which can cause oxygen deprivation in the brain and entire nervous system by decreasing blood circulation, slowing the delivery of oxygen and nutrients, by slowing the rate of food metabolism to nourish brain and nerve cells, by decreasing production of blood cells, by contributing to narrowing of arteries in atherosclerosis, and by limiting the amount of blood that reaches the brain. These physical changes caused by hypothyroidism contribute to decreased intellectual capabilities, poor memory, speech problems, decreased reasoning power, poor concentration, increased irritability, depression, anxiety, fear, insomnia, etc.

The following example will encourage you to read *Hypothyroidism* by Dr. Broda Barnes, M.D. and also *Solved the Riddle of Illness* by Dr. Stephen Langer, M.D. and overcome all the pitfalls of orthodox mismanagement of hypothyroidism. In this regard, I asked my friend if she had switched from synthetic thyroid medication to natural Armour thyroid. She replied, "No, my doctor told me that a recent blood thyroid test and Thyroid Stimulating Hormone Suppression test showed that the synthetic thyroid was working and that it was in my bloodstream." I explained that Synthroid contains only a synthetic form of T4, that Euthroid contains synthetic T4 and T3, and that, sure, the orthodox thyroid blood tests show the presence of synthetic T4 or T4/T3 and low TSH after taking synthetic thyroid medication.

I told my friend, "Your doctor tricked you and now you can easily understand how he did it. He gave you a pill made out of synthetic T4/T3 manmade things (not the complete natural thyroid hormone), tested you again later and found evidence of the T4/T3 things in your bloodstream, and then told you that this 'evidence' proved that the synthetic medication is effective. He probably went on to tell you that synthetic thyroid medication has been found to be more reliable than natural Armour thyroid."

What the Establishment doctor didn't tell my friend is that Dr. Barnes, after a lifetime of treating hypothyroidism successfully, states in his book that blood thyroid tests and the apparent effectiveness of synthetic thyroid medication are routinely misleading in that they typically show no thyroid problem when you actually have one. Consequently, Dr. Barnes concluded that blood thyroid tests and synthetic thyroid medication do not test and treat thyroid problems effectively and that the basal resting temperature test conquers these problems by testing thyroid function.

The bottom line is to determine if your thyroid gland is functioning well enough to keep your body temperature normal. This is important because your metabolic and enzyme systems work only within a very narrow range of temperature. If your body temperature is low, it causes hypothyroid symptoms and if too high, it causes hyperthyroid problems. This simple, proven resting temperature test bypasses all the concerns about trying to isolate and identify your thyroid hormone in its wholeness as created by God and it also circumvents all of the complicating factors, such as problems with low stomach acid, pituitary, hypothalamus, adrenals, gall bladder and pancreas.

Since modern medicine only pretends to offer a solution to all of these unanswered questions, bypass them by directly testing thyroid function with the temperature test.

Find an alternative medical doctor or osteopath who is ethical, who will listen and who will give you natural thyroid medication if you need it. He will understand that the basal temperature test is valid and reliable. He knows that the basal temperature runs below the normal range in hypothyroidism. The body thermostat of a thyroid deficient person may call for more heat but he does not have enough thyroid hormone to adequately oxidize or burn the food and stored nutrients to raise the body temperature to normal and this directly causes dysfunction and the seeds of disease in every organ in the body.

Based on 30 years of experience and many thousands of readings, Dr. Barnes, as outlined in his book *Hypothyroidism: The Unsuspected Illness,* has established that the normal underarm basal temperature is in the range of 97.8 to 98.2 degrees Fahrenheit if taken at rest for a full 10 minutes as instructed. A basal temperature below 97.8°F indicates hypothyroidism; a basal temperature above 98.2°F indicates hyperthyroidism, infection or a temporary disturbance.

The basal temperature at rest is different than the regular temperature taken when the person is active. The normal active temperature by mouth is 98.6°F ranging from 98.2°F to 99.0°F taken during the day or when you sit down in the doctor's office to have your temperature taken. The basal temperature by armpit is taken at rest during sleep or just before arising.

The basal temperature of an infant or child can be taken rectally for 2 minutes and since rectal temperatures are normally 1 degree higher, any temperature reading below 98.6⁰F can indicate hypothyroidism.

The basal temperature orally by mouth is usually avoided because an unknown infection, cold or sore throat could raise the oral temperature but usually not the armpit basal temperature. Some may want to take the basal temperature by armpit and by mouth to measure the basal temperature and to see if the oral temperature is raised indicating infection. Some people have chronic infection which they are not aware of and the difference between the basal armpit and basal oral temperatures could reflect an infection. The reasoning is that the armpit temperature is less affected by infection whereas the oral temperature is usually elevated during infection.

Men may take the Barnes basal temperature test any morning after a good night's rest. Women can take the basal temperature test on the 2nd or 3rd day after the beginning of menstrual blood flow when the monthly temperature fluctuations are normal. It is lowest during ovulation and slowly rises until just before the flow of blood when it is highest. It returns quickly to normal after blood flow begins. The basal temperature test can even be taken with fairly good accuracy on the 4th or later day of flow. Women can take their basal temperatures periodically to map out the temperature changes.

Before going to bed, shake down the thermometer below 96.0⁰F and place it on the bedstand near your reach for use first thing after awakening in the morning. Upon awakening, do not get up to go to the bathroom and do not stir around in bed. The whole idea is to take the temperature at rest. Calmly tuck the thermometer snugly under the arm under any bedclothes for 10 minutes by the clock or timer. Take a snooze for 10 minutes and then record the temperature in writing. To test for infection (not always conclusive), take a second thermometer shaken down the night before and place it in your mouth for another 10 minutes and record the termperature. For more information, also take the active armpit and oral temperature during the day about the same time of the day after the same type of activity to compare the basal temperature at rest with your regular active temperature. Repeat this process for three to seven days consecutively, wait for a week or two or longer and repeat the process. Do not rely on any temperature taken only one day because you may have done something wrong with the thermometer or you may have a different health problem which might affect the test.

Many commonly used drugs and even shampoo or skin antiseptics can upset test results. Problems with the pituitary, hypothalamus, adrenals, gall bladder, pancreas and other organs can affect thyroid function and the temperature test. Low stomach acid, hydrochloric acid, is a common cause of hypothyroidism and other health problems.

A basal temperature below 97.8°F indicates hypothyroidism and a basal temperature above 98.2°F indicates hyperthyroidism or possible infection.

A history of hiatal hernia and low hydrochloric stomach acid can also suggest a diagnosis of hypothyroidism. Vagus nerve interference in hiatal hernia can cause hypothyroidism and also low hydrochloric stomach acid.

Correcting thyroid deficiency and over 120 of its symptoms can be done effectively, inexpensively and safely by taking natural Armour brand thyroid, a prescription drug made from desiccated thyroid glands of cattle.

Improvements in symptoms may take one to twelve months after starting medication and persons with hypothyroidism will need to take the thyroid medication indefinitely. Since it takes a long time for thyroid medication to relieve symptoms and since the average person is lax about taking medication, the usual mistake is to stop taking the thyroid tablets.

Armour brand thyroid medication has been found superior to generic brands and synthetic thyroid. Patients treated with Armour brand responded in cases where generic and synthetic brands did not.

In addition, eat dulse seaweed or take kelp tablets daily to provide iodine which is used by the thyroid gland to manufacture thyroid hormone. If your body is not producing adequate hydrochloric acid, you may need to take this stomach acid in tablet form to help correct thyroid function. You may need to get diagnosis and treatment of hiatal hernia which is associated with hypothyroidism. Also recommended are chiropractic adjustments of cervical vertebra 5, 6, 7, thoracic 11 and 12 and lumbar 1 to normalize the nerve supply to the thyroid gland and related organs.

KIDNEY PROBLEMS CAUSE LOW BACK PROBLEMS

Most low back problems are caused or aggravated by a toxic and inflamed kidney condition as a consequence of the patient's intolerance to what he is eating and drinking and his bad habits. The key to solving the low back problem therefore is to eliminate the food, drinks and bad habits irritating the kidneys and low back muscles.

The kidneys, one of the most important eliminative organs, become overworked, fatigued, inflamed and compromised on a chronic day-to-day year-after-year basis from toxins and acids in foods, drinks and bad habits. Dairy, coffee, alcohol, drugs, medical drugs, smoking, not drinking sufficient amounts of water and eating too much meat are the most common causes of kidney toxicity and low back problems.

Other causes of kidney-low back pain and stiffness are: too much frozen or canned orange juice loaded with chemicals not even listed as ingredients; ham, bacon, sausage, pork roast, cold cuts, tuna, mackerel, shrimp, lobster, clams, oysters and other unclean meats and fish; too much meat in general; sugar; too many fruits or juices; processed and junk foods; food and environmental allergies; candidiasis and parasites; hypothyroidism; systemic toxicity; emotional stress; excess sex; and anything causing too much toxicity and acidity requiring elimination by the kidneys, especially when this type of self-afflicted poisoning has been going on for many years.

Day in day out, the kidneys are called upon to filter the blood and eliminate through the urine all of these diet and habit related metabolic toxins which cause irritation, congestion, inflammation and deterioration of the kidneys and the surrounding tissues.

The resulting inflammation, edema, swelling, and toxicity and free radical pathology spreads from the kidneys to the spinal nerves supplying the kidneys themselves and the nearby muscles, especially the psoas muscles. Called the kidney muscles, the psoas and iliopsoas become irritated, contract and literally pull the lumbars, sacro-iliac, hips and knees out of alignment and fixating them causing most low back stiffness, pain and chronic degenerative arthritic changes. I call this condition the toxic kidney-low back pain syndrome.

The symptoms of toxic kidney-low back pain syndrome are low back, sacroiliac, hip and knee stiffness and pain; sciatica pain running down one or both legs; congestion, crystals, heat or coldness, muscle contractions, pain and a clammy feeling of the skin alongside the spine in the area of the kidneys; general edema especially around the lumbo-sacral area; circles or bags under the eyes; abdominal and groin pain from the contracted psoas muscles; kidney stones; bladder and urinary problems and frequent infections; excess urination; female complaints; sexual problems; and lower colon problems.

Generally, the condition becomes progressively worse as the kidneys deteriorate and the kidney muscles pull the spine, pelvis, hips and knees out of alignment and fixate them. Spinal nerve irritation to the kidneys and psoas muscles cause more kidney inflammation and deterioration, more psoas muscle contraction and more toxic kidney-low back pain syndrome symptoms.

Toxic kidney-low back pain syndrome combined with systemic toxicity, free radical pathology and other underlying metabolic disorders may be a primary cause of chronic conditions such as degenerative joint disease, disc problems, arthritis and other degenerative changes of the low back spine, sacroiliac, hips and knees.

The Establishment doctor will usually wrongfully blame the patient's low back problems on a lifting or work related injury, accident or some mysterious degenerative disease which, according to their ideological rationalizations, has no cause or cure. Such a superficial diagnosis never identifies the unhealthful foods, drinks and bad habits as the primary cause of weakness and degenerative changes of the kidney, the kidney spinal muscles and spine, sacroiliac, hips and knees.

What you and your doctor may be reluctant to admit is that your foods, drinks and bad habits over a long period of time have created kidney problems and inflammation and weakness in the low back area making it more susceptible to degenerative changes and injury from trauma.

Many people do not know that unhealthful foods and bad habits cause back problems but when they first hear about this connection, they tend to ignore and minimize it because it is far easier and more convenient to blame the low back problem on a lifting injury or some other accident than go to the trouble of changing to a healthful lifestyle and giving up the foods and habits which they like but makes them sick.

Some people with diet and habit related kidney problems do not have obvious low back pain but closer examination by deep palpation of the kidney place and the abdominal psoas muscles reveals stiffness, limited range of motion, congestion, crystals, hardness and pain. These are the type who say they are healthy, have no pain with light palpation and don't need to change their diet or give up alcohol, smoking, coffee, dairy, etc. They will be first to blame a future low back problem on some lifting injury, turning the wrong way, etc. and never consider closing their mouths to unhealthful foods, drinks and bad habits.

Nevertheless, a good palpation examination and x-rays will reveal degenerative changes caused by the wrong foods and habits. After several treatments, excessively hard and stiff bodies relax a little allowing the person to actually feel where it hurts.

For those of you who are willing to clean up your diet and lifestyle, your body and blood system will detoxify and the kidney muscles will stop fixating and pulling your spine, sacroiliac, hips and knees out of alignment allowing your back troubles to melt away. Old injuries and even degenerative changes will start to heal perhaps for the first time in your life.

Correct other underlying causes of low back stiffness and pain by following through with a complete detoxification and healing program and that includes your spiritual life which may be the most important cause of all your troubles. Identify and treat any hypothyroidism, systemic toxicity, free radical pathology, candidiasis, parasites, hiatal hernia and other metabolic disorders which could be primary or secondary causes of low back problems.

Drink two to three quarts of pure water a day to help flush out the kidneys as a daily routine and especially when you have low back problems or other health difficulties.

For acute low back and related pain, such as sciatica, your body may be very toxic and acidic. It may be a good idea for you to eat an emergency temporary alkaline diet of cooked root and non-seed vegetables to help alkalize the system and hopefully help relieve the pain.

For acute problems, avoid meat, fish and egg protein until the condition improves to avoid overloading the kidneys.

Bowel constipation, whether you think you have it or not, can aggravate low back problems. Often a series of enemas or colonics can speed up your recovery. Take herbal laxatives and eat a diet that provides better bowel elimination.

Dairy is one of the worst foods for kidney-low back trouble as well as for most mid-back, shoulder and neck problems and dairy, especially cheese, is very constipating. Are you ready to give up dairy?

Electric hot packs which draw moisture to the skin or hot water packs applied 15 minutes over the kidneys, low back, abdomen and other areas of pain will help reduce muscle contraction and pain. Keep moving the hot pads around to a new place every 15 minutes. Falling asleep with the heating pad may cause the problems to get worse by actually causing contractions rather than relieving them. In certain inflamed conditions, ice packs are more helpful and in some cases, hot packs followed by ice packs are effective.

Exercise once a day to keep the kidney muscles relaxed and twice a day when you have low back stiffness and pain. Lie on your back, bring one knee up to your chest as far as possible without hurting yourself, breathe in and out for 5 deep breaths, relax the low back, hips and whole body, switch to the other side and repeat 5 times on both sides.

Then hold the knee with the opposite hand and torque the body by twisting the knee in to touch the floor on the other side keeping the shoulders as flat as possible. Breathe in and out for 5 deep breaths and relax as much as possible. Switch to the other side and repeat 5 times. You may at times hear the low back snap back into place.

The key idea in this series of exercises is to relax those contracted muscles which are pulling your skeletal frame out of alignment and fixating it. Breathing properly during the exercises and throughout the day will help you relax.

Get some massage and chiropractic adjustments to break the pattern, correct the nerve supply to the kidneys and speed up recovery.

In these circumstances, I always tell the patient that bodywork and chiropractic treatment may or may not make him feel better right away; that if he is very toxic, inflamed, swollen and supersensitive to pain, treatment may even make him feel worse temporarily or his body may not be ready to relax enough to be adjusted and mobilized; that he may need to detoxify before treatment is resumed; that he really needs to detoxify his body and kidneys; and that he will heal himself when and if he is willing to do what is necessary.

Most patients get better with a complete detoxification and healing program in 3 to 21 days and they often recover fully in 3 to 12 months when they improve their diet and eliminate bad habits thereby removing the primary cause of their low back problems.

LIVER AND GALL BLADDER PROBLEMS

Your liver is a complex, remarkable organ with the ability to regenerate to its original size when as much as half of it is surgically removed. It can function with only one-fifth its whole intact but why push your luck with an unhealthful diet, bad habits and medical drugs which damage it?

Your liver filters blood; phagocytizes (engulfs and eliminates) bacteria, toxins, antigen-antibody allergy complexes; synthesizes and secretes bile which is stored in the gall bladder; metabolizes carbohydrates, proteins and fats; manufactures billions of enzymes; stores vitamins and minerals; processes waste nitrogen into urea for excretion; produces red blood cells; synthesizes new protein body tissues; prepares fuel for oxidation and energy; stores excess nourishment for future use; forms coagulation factors, etc.

In short, your liver helps you get the nourishment out of the food you eat and it protects you by cleaning up the blood poisoned by unhealthful foods, bad habits, street drugs, alcohol, medical drugs, environmental pollutants, germs and toxins passed on to the liver from the intestines and colon.

Your gall bladder stores bile secreted by the liver and empties it into the duodenum of the small intestines where it emulsifies and breaks down fat globules into minute size and helps in absorption of fats by the small intestine.

Your liver and gall bladder can process just so much junk food, hot spices and altered oils and fats and they can filter and detoxify just so many germs, toxins, alcohol, etc. before they break down allowing these poisons to build up in the bloodstream and body tissues.

The price your liver pays for protecting you from what you put into your mouth is damage, fatty infiltration, congestion, sluggishness, enlargement, degeneration, infection and impaired function which leads to illness, disease and death.

Toxic or sluggish liver and gall bladder is in fact an important valid clinical entity despite what your Establishment doctor says and does to make them even more toxic and sluggish. The average person has some liver damage from self-induced abuse. Over-indulgence in foods, alcohol and other bad habits can deplete the alkalinity and sodium causing the liver cells to die and form scar tissue called cirrhosis.

Intestinal bacteria play a significant role in causing cirrhosis, liver damage and pancreatitis according to Nolan, Grune, Liehr, Camara, Broitman and others. Now your orthodox doctor will deny this by falsely claiming that intestinal bacteria and toxins stay inside the intestines until they are eliminated and do not pass through the intestinal wall into the bloodstream.

Unhealthful foods and bad habits toxify the intestines and break down the protective immunity in the intestinal walls causing them to become leaky thereby allowing intestinal toxins and bacteria to readily pass through the wall into the bloodstream. The portal vein then carries the poisons and germs to the liver for detoxification and phagocytosis but not before causing direct free radical damage to liver tissue and gall bladder stasis.

The immune factors in the intestinal wall are the first line of defense to keep unwanted toxins and germs in the intestines and out of the bloodstream and liver. When the intestinal walls fail because of toxic overload from dietary abuse and unhealthful habits, the liver is the second line of defense but it soon fails also from toxic overload, allowing toxins, germs and free radicals to exit the liver not neutralized and then be carried by the bloodstream to all cells and tissues throughout the body causing damage, inflammation, edema, congestion, dysfunction, illness, degenerative and infectious disease and eventually death.

As a result of excess acid toxicity and insufficient alkalinity in the liver from nutrient poor processed and junk foods and bad habits, the bile becomes toxic and turns dark green or black. Toxic bile irritates and inflames the liver, bile ducts, gall bladder and duodenum and it can be regurgitated into the stomach and esophagus. It can burn the duodenum and cause frightening spasms often misdiagnosed as ulcers.

Much of the harmful toxic bile and related toxins are reabsorbed by the intestinal villi and returned to the bloodstream creating increasing levels of systemic toxicity all over the body.

In a circular fashion as more and more poisons from an unhealthful diet and bad habits enter the mouth, the liver and gall bladder become progressively more toxic and sluggish causing weakness, sharp stabbing pains in the liver and gall bladder area, gallstones, indigestion, inability to digest fats, gas, gastrointestinal distress, bitter taste, spasms, feeling of fullness, nausea, weakness, fatigue, spots before the eyes, cataracts, swollen ankles, pseudo heart attack symptoms, cold sweats, jaundice, hepatitis, itching, clay colored or dry, hard stools, constipation, varicose veins, phlebitis, hemorrhoids, headache, irritability and referred pain between the right shoulder blade and spine.

Anger overstimulates the production of bile or gall and reactivates liver and gall bladder problems; hence the term gall. If you don't believe this, the next time you get angry, feel your liver and gall bladder area below your right rib cage for pain.

Orthodox medical treatment of liver and gall bladder disease includes drugs, especially corticosteroids, surgical removal of the gall bladder for gallstones and very little and very inadequate dietary advice. Missing from medical treatment are detoxification, more complete dietary measures and nutritional and herbal supplements to protect the liver from damage.

Detoxification is the first initial step in the treatment of liver and gall bladder disease and any other disease. A good detoxification program should include a series of colonics or enemas and an herbal laxative every day for 7 days; then one per week and repeat the 7 day bowel cleansing program every 6 weeks until not needed to reduce the intestinal toxins and germs which poison and damage the liver and the rest of the body.

Note that orthodox treatment almost never includes bowel cleansing except maybe as part of the treatment for hepatic coma. This is a shame because bowel cleansing should be advised for all types of liver and gall bladder dysfunction to reduce toxic overload to the liver.

Antibiotics and steroids can cause candidiasis related toxicity and more toxic damage to the liver. Candidiasis and treatment for candidiasis are routinely ignored, minimized and ridiculed by orthodoxy and rarely considered in treatment of liver disease.

To treat liver and gall bladder disease, it is best to give the liver a rest by drinking lots of fresh vegetable juice, particularly beet, beet tops and parsley mixed with carrot juice.

Drink as much organic apple juice in between meals as possible to help soften any gallstones. Also in between meals mid-morning and mid-afternoon, take 2 tsp. di-sodium phospate in 4 oz. of hot water to stimulate the liver and gall bladder.

Drink 16 oz. of pure water with the juice of a fresh lemon to help flush out the liver, gall bladder, spleen, kidneys, bladder and intestines.

Eat light meals, drink 2 to 3 quarts of water a day and avoid all rich foods, strong spices and eliminate all free oils and fats. Temporarily, avoid seeds, nuts and anything oily.

Since free oils and fats, especially when rancid, are the most common source and cause of free radicals, be especially careful to eliminate all free oils and fats to prevent free radical damage to the liver.

In case of severe liver disease, avoid all animal protein for the first three weeks of treatment but do include complete vegetable proteins by combining whole grains with lentils because the liver requires high quality protein to repair liver damage. After three weeks, add white ocean fish and organically raised eggs twice a week. Organically raised beef and chicken liver are good if you can find them or take organic liver supplements.

If liver disease is not severe, add fish and eggs twice a week right away because animal protein is a higher quality protein than vegetable sources.

The following supplements and herbs are recommended to

stimulate bile production and bile flow, to protect liver tissue from inflammatory and free radical damage, to stimulate liver tissue repair and to stimulate liver macrophage Kupffer cells which can phagocytize as much as 99% of all bacteria entering the liver from the portal vein from the intestines.

Take choline 1 gram and L-methionine 2 grams per day and S-adenosylmethionine (SAM) 200 mg three times a day to protect the liver from toxic damage. In case of alcohol-induced fatty liver disease, take L-carnitine 500 mg three times a day to normalize fatty acid infiltration of the liver. Take desiccated neonatal liver extract 500 mg three times a day to build up the liver.

Take vitamin C 3 to 10 grams daily or to bowel tolerance to stimulate detoxification and antibiotic activity in the liver.

Dandelion herb is regarded as one of the best liver remedies to enhance the production and flow of bile. Take dandelion root 4 grams or dandelion extract 250 to 500 mg three times a day.

Milk thistle herb containing silymarin is one of the most potent liver protection substances known to protect the liver from free radical damage by acting as an antioxidant. Silymarin is many times more potent as an antioxidant than vitamin E and C, zinc and selenium. Milk thistle also protects the liver by inhibiting the production of leukotriene, an inflammatory allergic mediator and milk thistle has the amazing ability to stimulate protein synthesis in the production of new liver cells to replace the damaged old ones. Take milk thistle 350 to 700 mg or silymarin extract 70 to 140 mg three times a day.

Take Goldenseal 1 gram daily to stimulate bile flow, improve symptoms of chronic gall bladder disease and fight infection.

Licorice containing glycyrrhin has been shown by double blind studies in Japan to be quite effective in treating viral hepatitis but should be monitored by a nutritional doctor to avoid any problems with licorice induced pseudo-aldosteronism.

Most important: silymarin and dandelion.

After two weeks of the above regimen, you may consider flushing out the gall bladder under supervision of your doctor. Your medical doctor should test you to determine if you have gallstones and if they are small enough to safely pass from the gall bladder.

Large gallstones can get stuck in the bile duct causing much pain and even death. Therefore, the following information is for your education only and must be approved by your nutritional medical doctor. Do not attempt this procedure without proper diagnosis and supervision.

The liver and gall bladder treatment program should prepare you for the gall bladder flush using lemon juice and olive oil. The day before and the day of the treatment, eat lightly, eat at least 16 oz. of whole kernel corn for its fiber content to help clean out the colon, take a colonic or enema, drink as much apple juice as possible, take 2 tsp. di-sodium phosphate in 4 oz. hot water between meals mid-morning and mid-afternoon and an extra time 2 hours after dinner. At bedtime, take a strong herbal laxative.

Then on the day of treatment at bedtime, mix ½ cup fresh lemon juice and ½ cup olive oil and drink. Brush your teeth to get the nasty taste out of your mouth and fight off any nausea. Go to bed right away and lie on your right side and go to sleep. If you wake up in a different position, return to your right side.

Some may experience a lot of nausea or perhaps the need to vomit. Fight off nausea and vomiting to keep the lemon juice and oil in you all night if possible. Throw up if you have to but if you do, plan on repeating the procedure as soon as you can in the next couple of days.

In the morning, drink a little water and take 2 tsp. di-sodium phosphate with 4 oz. hot water. As soon as you feel like it, eat 8 to 16 oz. of whole kernel corn to stimulate bowel evacuation and it tends also to settle the stomach which is likely to be a little queasy. It is common to feel wiped out; therefore plan on resting. You may feel better right away but you may be tired. Rest and sleep as much as possible and drink lots of water, carrot juice and organic apple juice.

Insert a glycerine suppository to stimulate a bowel movement and try to have as many bowel movements as possible. About mid-morning, take a colonic or enema. Do not flush the toilet right away to give you time to inspect the contents for a green powder or pellets which float in the water.

There is some controversy from orthodox medicine and other non-believers whether these green objects are really gallstones or simply olive oil fats. In any case, many people report relief from liver and gall bladder congestion and related symptoms by following these procedures. Repeat the procedure every six months or as needed.

Psychologically, all of us at some level hide from ourselves and we try to justify feelings of anger. The gall bladder flush helps wash away the anger but not the tendency to get angry again. In fact, we tend to return to the previous state of anger and distress unless we consciously control it by turning it over to God.

MEAT, FISH AND EGGS

Beef, veal, venison, lamb, mutton, poultry, eggs and fish are good for man provided they are not eaten in excess or contaminated by petrochemicals, pesticides, herbicides, antibiotics, hormones and germs. Only meat and poultry raised on uncontaminated home grown grains and grasses should be eaten. Marbled meat may taste good because of the high fat content but the marbling is a sign of a lack of calcium in the animal's diet. Most commercial animal and poultry feed contain chemicals not listed on the label.

Organically raised meat is not readily available and the cost is prohibitive for most people, although it is recommended that you bear the extra cost of clean meat if at all possible. Eating clean meat once or twice a week is far better and perhaps just as economical as eating low quality unclean meat more often when damage to your health and health costs of eating unclean meat are also considered.

Blood in meat is very toxic and should be removed by placing it in a large container and covering it with a salty brine by adding one-fourth cup non-iodized salt to each quart of water. Refrigerate and allow it to soak for 12 hours or longer depending on the size of the cut of meat. Roasts and larger cuts should soak 18 hours and ground meat should soak only 2 hours.

Pour off the brine water and cover the meat with water with no salt in it. Return the meat to the refrigerator to soak as long or longer than it did in the salt water. The fresh water removes the salt and blood and as the blood is drawn out, change the water every 4 to 6 hours to keep it fresh. Larger cuts should soak in plain water 24 to 36 hours and ground meats should soak 3 to 4 hours.

Restrict red meat to once a week or once every two weeks and rely more on eating fresh, clean fish. In general, fish or red meat should be eaten only once or twice a week. More fish and meat can be eaten on a temporary emergency basis to help repair the damage from broken bones, torn muscles and severe burns and drink 2 to 3 quarts of water to flush out the extra protein wastes.

Due to contamination of most red meat, white ocean fish is the best source of uncontaminated meat but unfortunately even ocean fish are becoming more and more polluted with chemicals and waste products which have already made most fresh inland water fish unfit for human consumption. About the only safe fresh inland water fish are unpolluted mountain stream trout, bass and salmon.

The clean fish include: mahimahi, cod, haddock, grouper, hake, herring, kipper, ling cod, mullet, pilchard, pollock, pompano, porgy, red snapper, rose fish, sardine, sea trout, shad, whiting, trout, bass and salmon. See unclean foods on page 52.

Eliminate all unclean meat and foods listed in the Bible. Pork and all pork products are especially unclean and very dangerous to eat. According to Dr. Hans Heinrich Reckeweg, M.D., pork contains poisonous substances called sutoxins, which cause many acute and degenerative diseases. Specifically, these disease causing poisons in pork are: cholesterol loaded macro-molecules causing increased muscular tension, arteriosclerosis and cancer; histamine and imidazole bodies causing skin diseases, herpes, eczema, itching, inflammatory responses, carbuncles, boils, moles, appendicitis, gallbladder inflammation and thrombophlebitis; growth hormones promoting inflammatory reactions, abnormal growth tendencies and cancer; fatty acids causing decreased muscular strength and abnormal increase in red blood cells; high sulphur substances causing hardening of the muscles, joint diseases, bone disorders, rheumatism and arthritis; oncogenic agents causing cancer; influenza viruses causing flu and meningitis, encephalitis and other neurological diseases, sometimes fatal. Read "The Adverse Influence of Pork Consumption on Health" by Dr. Reckeweg, "Biological Therapy," Vol. 1, November 2, 1983 available by writing to Menaco Publishing Company, P.O. Box

13677, Albuquerque, NM 87192.

Apologists for the standard unhealthful American diet and propagandists for the processed food industry, especially the pork industry would have you believe that Jesus Christ did away with all the restrictions on clean and unclean foods but this is not true at all. In Mark 7:19, Christ did lift the veil of superstition, custom, tradition and pagan ritual surrounding food and its preparation but He DID NOT give you a prescription to eat unclean foods. Christ eliminated the superstition around food but He did not eliminate the inherent poisons in pork, scavenger seafood, insects and other contaminated food which cause toxicity, degeneration, cancer and death.

The vision that Peter saw in Acts 10 and 11 does not mean that the unclean food laws were lifted; these Bible passages affirm that both Gentiles and non-Gentiles can become Christians.

Hebrews 9:10 states that the shed blood of Jesus did away with animal blood sacrifices and this does not in any way give you permission to eat rats, catfish and other unclean foods.

Romans 14 says it is wrong to judge and condemn a person for what he eats. A Christian can eat unclean foods because what we eat does not determine our relationship to God but why eat unclean foods? Which is better? Being a sick Christian or a healthy Christian?

Hebrews 13:9 warns us not to get fanatical about food because fanaticism will not get you into the kingdom of God. Similarly, it is also not a good idea to get fanatical about your "right" as a Christian to eat "all of God's creatures" because the Bible does not say to eat all of God's unclean creatures.

First Corinthians 8 and 10:25-33 refers to not offending others concerning meat offered as a sacrifice or periodically accepting unclean meat from someone but does not give you the excuse to eat unclean foods on a regular basis.

Personally, I would decline eating unclean food offered to me by anyone for any reason but I would try to do it as nicely as possible. Be wary of those individuals and pastors who use the Bible to justify their unhealthful eating habits.

For those of you who love tuna but want to avoid it because it is unclean, note that canned salmon, sardine and pilchard are a good substitute for canned tuna. Storing clean fish as survival foods in these troubled times seems to be a good idea.

Eggs from chickens raised on uncontaminated organic feed and table scraps are good food despite what you may have been told about avoiding the cholesterol in eggs. Eggs do have cholesterol in the yolk but the white has lecithin which emulsifies the cholesterol. Furthermore, free radical pathology not cholesterol is the major cause of arteriosclerosis and cardiovascular disease.

Free radicals from oils and fats and other sources injure the walls of the blood vessels and the body sends cholesterol and plaque to cover up the lesions or sores caused by free radical damage. Therefore, free radicals are the cause of vascular and heart disease and cholesterol is only the symptom.

Why remove cholesterol by not eating eggs and red meat when you should eliminate oils, fats, dairy and other sources of free radicals instead? Does it make any sense to stop eating eggs and to listen to the bad advice of recommending cholesterol-free vegetable oils which cause free radical damage? The low cholesterol fad popularized by the processed food industry-medical monopoly axis sells a lot of vegetable oil, synthetic fats, low fat dairy, etc. but does it make you healthy and penny wise?

A person can safely eat eggs every day without any problems if he needed that much protein but he doesn't. Eat eggs once or twice a week and enjoy them! The best way to cook eggs is to leave the yolk and white intact to decrease production of free radicals when the two are mixed before cooking. Cakes, cookies, bread, etc. made with eggs are not the best way to eat eggs. To minimize free radicals, eat eggs boiled, poached or sunnyside up.

Raw eggs are good food and according to Dr. Dean Burk, do not worry about causing a biotin deficiency said to be caused by eating raw eggs. In any case, you can take biotin supplements to put your mind at ease.

Vegetarianism is recommended on a temporary basis for the person who eats too much meat and is toxic and constipated, especially those with kidney problems. Certain meat-eaters need a rest from meat because their bodies are overly hard, congested and toxic and unable to feel deep palpation along the spine due to excessive nerve irritation and pain simply turned off as a protective measure. When you don't listen to your body, it stops sending pain signals to wake you up. It goes to sleep and so do you, your mind and your sensitivity and awareness to the environment, nature and social interchange.

Wake up and clean up your body by eliminating red meat for one to six months or completely. A temporary meat-free vegetarian diet is indicated for kidney disease in the acute stage. When the health crisis is over, eat white ocean fish and eggs once or twice a week. Thereafter, limit red meat and only eat it from animals raised on organically raised grains and grasses.

Liver disease requires high quality animal protein for proper tissue regeneration and healing and these requirements can be met by eating fish and eggs. In acute liver disease and toxicity, temporarily eliminate all animal protein until the acute stage has passed and then eat clean fish and eggs once or twice a week to help regenerate the liver.

Vegetarians who insist on not eating fish and eggs should at least take vitamin B-12, Bio-Therapeutics Aqueous Liver Extract Capsules (call 800-553-2370) and complete balanced amino acid supplements, especially if they have liver problems.

NUT-SEED MILK

almonds	fresh or dried coconut
walnuts	pumpkin seeds
cashews	sunflower seeds
macadamia	flax seeds
	other nuts and seeds

Select nuts and seeds and grind them in a small coffee grinder, Cusinart kitchen machine or Vita Mix. Grind only the amount needed to maintain freshness. The best method is to soak the seeds or nuts overnight, discard the water and blend into milk.

Place ½ cup ground seeds and nuts in a blender and blend until smooth with water and several ice cubes. Add honey, vanilla and salt to taste. Try adding dates. Add as much water as you like, usually about 2 cups. Saves in the refrigerator for 1 or 2 days.

Larger amounts can be made. If you like it smooth, strain using a cotton baby diaper. Buy a dozen cotton baby diapers, launder them and store them in a plastic bag for use as straining cloths.

For holidays or special occasions, spice up the nut-seed milk by adding dates and allspice, cinnamon, honey, vanilla and salt. Add raw eggs for eggnog.

OILS AND FATS — NUMBER ONE CAUSE OF DISEASE AND DEATH

The wrong kind of oils and fats, especially the processed oils and fats altered by heat, liquification and hydrogenation, are the worst food you can eat and the number one cause of disease and death. This means that you might consider eliminating from your diet all the vegetable oil, salad dressing, mayonnaise, fried foods and the foods made from hydrogenated oils, such as margarine, shortening, peanut butter, baked goods, ice cream, chocolate, candy, potato chips and other chips. They taste good but they are killing you.

The programmed consumption of processed oils and fats, a $60 billion business protected by the corrupt Food and Drug Administration, is the most important cause of arteriosclerosis, stroke and heart attack, the number one cause of death in the United States killing over one and a half million people each year and also a leading cause of cancer, the number two cause of death killing over one half million people annually.

As a result of a massive campaign by the processed food industry and government spokesmen to foist processed foods on the American public, total consumption of modified oils and fats between 1900 and 1980 increased, rising from 32 percent of daily calories to 42 percent and is still rising every year. Some people eat as much as 70% of daily calories in oils and fats. Did you know that excess calories from refined sugars and refined starches (white flour, white rice, white pasta) in the diet are transformed into the saturated, hard, sticky kind of fat?

In addition to eating too many oils and fats and too many refined carbohydrates which turn into fat, you are eating the wrong kind of oils and fats from foods lacking in essential fatty acids. Most people eat non-essential oils and fats and very little, if any, essential oils and fats. This is why our teenagers develop arteriosclerosis and why over half the adult population has cardiovascular diseases, arthritis, cancer or some other degenerative disease, which could be prevented if our Establishment doctors, registered dietitians, teachers, lawyers, politicians and bureaucrats and the controlled media were not in the pocket of the processed food and medical drug industries.

Research indicates that we need to bring our oil and fat consumption down to 15 to 20% of total daily calories and one-third of those oils and fats should be the omega 6 linoleic, omega 3 linolenic, EPA and GLA essential fatty acids. Less than 10% of daily calories in oils and fats, especially when deficient in the essential kind, causes many health problems and diseases. In short, too much fat, the wrong kind of fat and not enough of the right kind of fat cause degeneration and disease.

Linoleic and linolenic acid are essential fatty acids, which means they are necessary for life, the body cannot make them and we must get them from food sources. The minimum daily requirement for linoleic acid is 3 grams; the optimum dose is between 10 and 30 grams daily; and the therapeutic dose for treatment of degenerative diseases is 60 grams daily with no known toxic effects. The minimum daily requirement for linolenic acid is 1.5 grams; the optimum dose is 6 grams daily; and the therapeutic dose is up to 60 grams daily.

The functions of omega 6 linoleic and omega 3 linolenic fatty acids are impressive and underscore the fact that these essential fats are the most important food for a healthy body. Linoleic and linolenic essential fats are involved with the production of life energy in the body from food substances, the transfer of oxygen from the air in the lungs, through the capillary wall into the blood plasma, across the red blood cell membrane to the hemoglobin, which then carries the oxygen to all body cells; holding oxygen in the cell membrane as a barrier to viruses and bacteria; production of the red blood pigment hemoglobin; form a structural part of all cell membranes governing the movement of substances in and out of the cells; form a structural component of organelles within the cell which determine cellular function; substantially shorten the recovery time of fatigued muscles after exercise by facilitating the conversion of lactic acid to water and carbon dioxide; the secretion of all hormones and juices from the glands; are precursors of prostaglandins, which regulate many functions, such as involuntary muscle contractions, lower blood pressure, relax coronary arteries, inhibit blood platelet stickiness; growth enhancing; increase the metabolic rate of burning fat into energy and waste products; keep body fat deposits fluid; generating electrical currents that make the heart beat; and are the highest source of energy in nutrition.

The best sources of essential oils are fresh fish, frozen fish, fish liver oil capsules, walnuts, soybeans and the seeds of flax, sesame, pumpkin and sunflower. Beef, mutton, pork, cheese and butter are poor sources of essential oils. Heat and cold processing of common liquid vegeatable oils destroys most or all of its essential oils, and this is another reason why you should eat the whole food, such as freshly ground or creamed seeds, with its essential oils still intact safely inside individual fat cells.

Salmon, trout, sardines, mahimahi, bass, cod, halibut and other clean fish contains large quantities of essential fatty acids, especially the liver of salmon, cod and other cold water fish, and these are the source of fish liver oil, best taken in the capsule form. These fish liver oils contain EPA and DHA essential fatty acids, which clean up the arteries and prevent fatty degeneration. A healthy body can slowly manufacture both EPA and DHA from linolenic acid but fatty degeneration in an unhealthy body impairs the ability to manufacture EPA and DHA. Furthermore, most people do not eat foods with enough linolenic acid in the first place.

Gamma linolenic acid is a special essential fatty acid found in mother's milk and the seeds of borage and primrose flowers and healthy bodies can make it from essential linolenic acid but unhealthy bodies cannot. GLA is a precursor of the beneficial prostaglandins important in so many metabolic functions, including burning fats. It may appear contradictory but GLA, EPA, linolenic and linoleic essential oils increase the metabolic rate and help you lose weight.

The symptoms of essential fatty acid deficiency include: skin eruptions, acne, loss of hair, liver degeneration, behavioral disturbances, kidney degeneration, excessive water loss through the skin accompanied by thirst, drying up of glands, susceptibility to infections, failure of wound healing, sterility in males, miscarriage, arthritis, cancer, cardiovascular disease, retardation of growth, weakness, poor vision, impaired learning ability, motor incoordination, tingling in arms and legs, bowel toxicity, constipation, poor assimilation of nutrients, systemic toxicity, free radical pathology, and cellular degeneration, which is a primary cause of all degenerative diseases. Again, too little of the right essential oils and fats and too many of the wrong non-essential oils and fats cause these health problems.

Deficiency of linolenic acid during fetal development and early infancy can cause permanent learning disability and underlie the importance for women during pregnancy and for nursing mothers to eat foods containing lots of essential fatty acids. Mothers need to nurse their babies to provide them with the gamma linolenic essential fatty acids.

Clearly it is a criminal negligence for orthodox medical doctors and Establishment dietitians to recommend a diet deficient in essential fats and oils and it should be a mandatory prison term for minimizing breast feeding and for recommending baby formulas, which contain no essential fatty acids, a sure way to make your baby slow or retarded.

Cold pressed oil is a little better than heat processed oil but neither is natural and as with all free oils removed from their source, both cold and heat processed polyunsaturated vegetable oils should be eliminated from the diet.

In the supermarket the label on safflower, corn, olive, canola and other vegetable oils reads "Natural" but it should read, "A highly processed, unnatural free oil known to cause indigestion, poor assimilation, constipation, malnutrition, free radical pathology, cardiovascular disease, cancer, disease and death." Wouldn't sell much oil but it would save many lives.

Free oils (liquid oils) extracted from seeds, nuts, grains and olives are harmful to the body. This vital health message about the dangers of free oil was delivered over 100 years ago but was withheld by the food and drug industry and the medical industry, the number one and number two money-making industries in America. You were not told that all free oil in polyunsaturated vegetable oil, shortening, salad dressing, mayonnaise, peanut butter, gravy, margarine, butter, lard, fries and the thousands of processed foods containing free oils could make you sick.

In 1877, Dr. John Harvey Kellogg, a great physician, early Seventh-Day Adventist health reformer and brother to the founder of the Kellogg cereal company, wrote, "The objection is not against fat, per se, but against taking it in a free state. When taken in the form in which nature presents them enclosed in cells in such vegetable foods as corn, oatmeal, nut and some fruit, fats are a wholesome and nutritious element of food.

"It is only when separated from the other elements and taken in a free state that they become unwholesome . . . (and) become a means of producing disturbance of the digestive function. It makes little or no difference so far as the interference with digestion is concerned whether the fat is animal or vegetable."

Free oils and fats coat everything you eat with a film of oil which prevents proper digestion causing gastrointestinal upset, putrefaction, gas, poor assimilation, constipation, toxicity and degenerative disease. Fats and oils are digested in the small intestine whereas carbohydrates and proteins are digested in the stomach and small intestine and, of course, the digestion of carbohydrates begins in the mouth by the action of digestive enzymes in your saliva.

A film of free oil or fat covering the surface of ingested carbohydrates and proteins in your stomach puts up an unnatural physical barrier of oil slick between the foods and the digestive acids and enzymes which break down the food for digestion. Adequate digestion of these carbohyudrates and proteins is thereby delayed up to 20 hours causing putrefaction, gas and toxic by-products.

The consequences in the small intestine are more indigestion, more decay, more gas, more toxins and poor assimilation of nutrients. The nutrients are there but by now they are partially decomposed and not broken down in a form which allows their proper absorption and assimilation into the bloodstream and lymph system. This may help explain why you may have nutritional deficiencies even when you eat a lot of "good" food and why you crave more food to make up for your inability to get the energy out of the foods you ate previously.

Decaying food matter does not provide good nutrition but it does make good food for millions of germs and candida yeast organisms, which along with inflammatory agents, free radicals and immune factors inflame and irritate the walls of the small intestine. The resulting pain and bloating is what you feel when you deeply palpate your small intestines. If you have asked yourself what is causing all that pain and congestion in your abdomen, now you know.

The rotting food, toxins, inflammatory and immune factors, free radicals, parasites and germs are absorbed by the villi of the small intestine into the bloodstream and lymph system and carried via the portal vein to the liver for metabolism and detoxification or by the lymph vessels to all parts of the body.

Therefore, the consequences of eating free oils and fats and other unhealthful food are indigestion, gas, poor assimilation, nutritional deficiencies and malnutrition in spite of eating large quantities of food, abnormal craving of food, weakness, fatigue, constipation, systemic toxicity, free radical pathology, infection, inflammation, water retention, swelling, congestion, achiness, painful joints, migrating pain, allergy, lowered resistance to disease, cardiovascular disease, arthritis, cancer and other degenerative diseases.

In addition to the problem with oil slick around the foods you eat, what in free oils and fats causes so many of the above health problems? Free radicals. Peroxidized oils and fats are by far the most common and most dangerous source of free radical pathology. Oils and fats become peroxidized and transformed into free radicals upon exposure to air while being heated and fat in the body also oxidizes into toxic free radical peroxides.

Free radicals are unstable chemicals which occur naturally in the body and are also found in oils and fats, unhealthful foods and pollutants. These free radicals are highly reactive and increase exponentially unless controlled by: naturally occuring superoxide dismutase enzymes produced by the liver, by eating a healthful diet, by eliminating alcohol, cigarettes, coffee, soft drinks and street drugs and by living, breathing and working in a clean environment.

Excess free radical molecules trigger chain reactions that damage cell membranes, alter the cell's genetic material, literally eat up connective tissue around joints, strip the protective lining from nerve cells and cause thousands of other inflammatory, nerve and degenerative processes.

Polyunsaturated vegetable oils, so highly recommended by your orthodox doctor, are most easily oxidized and transformed into deadly free radicals, especially when used over and over to cook French fries and other junk foods. Hydrogenated oils, found in margarine, shortening, peanut butter and many processed foods are also dangerous sources of free radical pathology.

Saturated fats, found in butter and animal fats, are less easily peroxidized into free radicals but will oxidize if the temperature is too high as in broiling and grilling.

You are familiar with the term rancid oil but did you know that rancid oil is a problem not only due to its offensive odor and taste but also because it produces millions of free radicals which damage the body and cause disease?

The processed food industry attempts to reduce rancidity and free radicals and increase shelf life by super heating, bleaching and filtering out the substances responsible for making oil rancid. But what is left is a clear, lifeless, tasteless, marketable "oil" which has very little real nutritional value plus it is still rancid and a serious source of free radical pathology.

All free oils oxidize, become rancid and form free radicals just as soon as they are heat or cold processed. There is no such thing as a natural, fresh free oil. It is virtually impossible to remove oil from a seed, nut or grain under conditions of no oxygen or no light to prevent oxidation.

Based on these facts, all free oils as marketed now should be outlawed. If any free oils and fats were allowed at all, they would be stamped with a very short expiration date, refrigerated, stored in nitrogen packed bottles, preserved with vitamin E and herbal antioxidants and put in bottles impervious to the damaging effects of light.

But what passes now for "natural" free oil and fat is really an invitation to eat yourself into an early grave. Think about this the next time you enjoy French fries, fried foods, salad dressing, margarine and processed foods.

Free radical damage, not cholesterol, causes atherosclerosis and cardiovascular disease. Eating free oils and other unhealthful foods produces free radicals which, among other things, damages the walls of your blood vessels. As a protective measure, your body tries to heal the free radical lesions in the blood vessels by depositing plaque containing mostly cholesterol, calcium and scar tissue in an attempt to cover up the lesions caused by free radical pathology.

Wissler, a medical researcher, has found that vegetable oil reduces blood cholesterol. However, the cholesterol is not eliminated from the body but instead merely driven into the walls of the arteries causing worse atherosclerosis or hardening of the arteries, a prelude to arteriosclerosis, stroke and heart disease which now kills 50 percent of all Americans. He reported that peanut oil was the worst followed by butter and corn oil.

Meyer found that both unsaturated vegetable oils and saturated animal fats cause red blood cells to clump together cutting off oxygen to the tissues. Swank discovered that a high fat meal given to hamsters caused a 62 percent decrease in the amount of oxygen to the brain.

One study showed that safflower, corn, olive and other so-called natural oils were actually carcinogenic. Sweeney reported that a group of normal, healthy college men developed diabetes when fed a high fat diet. Singh found that 72 percent of adult onset diabetics were able to go off their insulin entirely by eating a low fat diet.

Blankernhorn found that when all major risk factors for atherosclerosis are taken into account — age, smoking, blood pressure and cholesterol — the more fat a person eats, the greater is his risk of developing cardiovascular disease. Subjects with the highest intake of fat, constituted 34 percent or more of their diet, were 12 times more likely to develop new lesions than men with the lowest intake of fat, constituting 23 percent or less of their diet. Coconut and palm oils were the worst.

A high intake of olive oil, a monounsaturated fat, produced a 5-fold risk of atherosclerosis, which was lower than the 12-fold risk associated with polyunsaturated oils. This means that olive oil is the lesser of two evils, i.e., better than polyunsaturated but both types of free oil should be avoided.

Your orthodox doctor seems to have no qualms about recommending trans fatty acids found in margarine, peanut butter, mayonnaise, salad oil and other hydrogenated processed foods. But does he tell you that trans fatty acids damage, sicken and destroy cells by making the cell membrane more permeable and leaky, disrupt the function of essential fatty acids and basic chemical reactions in the body which interfere and limit all life functions, including healthy nerve transmission, cell division, coordination, sensory mechanisms, muscle tone in the walls of the arteries, heartbeat, blood pressure, blood stickiness and clotting, mental balance and vitality? Why would any doctor do this to you?

European countries, less controlled by the United States Food and Drug Administration, the medical drug and processed food industry and the orthodox medical monopoly in America, know just how dangerous trans fats are and allow only a fraction of 1% trans fats in processed foods. The medical Establishment, which euphemistically calls itself modern medicine, recommends margarine, mayonnaise and other altered oils and fats containing up to 70% trans fats, which are proven carcinogens and causes of cardiovascular disease. Is "modern" medicine killing or curing us?

The average orthodox medical doctor or nutritionist and the heart disease charity organizations may mislead you about the dangers of trans fatty acids and free radicals and the lack of essential fatty acids in most oils and fats by half-truths. The party line is simply: eliminate total oils and fats to 30 percent of daily calories but don't worry about processed altered oils and fats, trans fatty acids, free radicals, essential fatty acids, metabolism, nutrition, cell wall permeability, body electromagnetism, life functions, disease and death.

What good comes from recommending a reduction in total calories in the diet from fats to 30 percent, 20 percent or even 10 percent when you are not told to avoid all free oils and fats, hydrogenated oils, trans fats and other altered oils and fats?

Note that natural oils and fats are necessary for every metabolic function in the body. A diet with no oils and fats or less than 10 percent of total calories can cause poor absorption and deficiencies of the oil soluble vitamins A, D, E and K and also deficiencies of essential linoleic and linolenic acids associated with cancer. On the other hand, diets high in oils, fats and proteins can cause kidney damage, cardiovascular problems, cancer and other degenerative diseases.

Why make yourself sick trying to lose weight by giving up all oils and fats or by eating mostly oils, fats and protein? Fad diets may help you lose weight but you are likely to regain all those extra pounds unless you adopt a sensible lifetime natural diet which will give you long term weight control.

Despite medical monopoly claims to the contrary, intravenous chelation therapy neutralizes free radicals, prevents and even reverses free radical damage in stroke, heart disease, cancer and other degenerative diseases. Eating properly will prevent future free radical pathology. See chapter on Free Radical Pathology.

Eliminate all free oils and fats from the diet, eat only clean foods and especially avoid pork, bacon, sausage, pork chops, pork roast and lard and drink 2 to 3 quarts of water a day. Saute without free oils or butter by using liquid aminos, water or a combination of both. Put a little butter on baking pans to prevent sticking. Use salad dressing with no free oils made from creamed nuts, seeds, olives and avocados. Do not allow any situation or anyone, including yourself, to encourage you to eat otherwise.

You will get all the oils you need from fish, fish liver oil capsules, raw seeds and nuts, fresh corn on the cob, avocado and cooked grains.

The very best foods contain one-third to one-half of their fatty acids as essential fatty acids, linoleic and linolenic and they are fish and the fresh whole seeds of flax, sunflower, pumpkin and sesame. Try seed milk made from a combination of all of these important foods simply by blending them together with pure water, 1 ice cube and perhaps a little sea salt, vanilla and honey or rice syrup. Freshly grind flax, pumpkin, sunflower or sesame seeds and mix with a little water, fresh lemon juice, onion or garlic powder, sea salt, cayenne pepper and sometimes with cashew spread. Use as a sandwich and add fresh sprouts.

Include fresh fish, fish liver oil capsules and flax, sunflower, pumpkin and sesame seeds in your diet because their high level of essential linolenic and linoleic acids will improve dry skin, infant eczema, teenage and adult acne and constipation. There is also some evidence these foods are helpful in the treatment of cancer.

Beef, mutton, pork, cheese and butter are not good sources of the essential fatty acids. Beef contains only 2 percent as essential fatty acids and the long term consumption of beef inhibits the function of the essential linoleic acid in the body and is actually an essential fatty acid robber.

Chicken and turkey (not the skin) are a good source of linoleic essential oils but only eat the range fed, organic variety. Almost all chickens and turkeys raised on processed feed and water loaded with pesticides, herbicides, tranquilizers, antibiotics and growth hormones develop cancer and other diseases as a consequence of their unhealthful manmade, chemicalized lifestyle.

The oil in fresh, whole flax seed is the richest of all food sources of essential fatty acids containing 50 to 60 percent of linolenic acid and 15 to 25 percent of linoleic acid.

Make a flax shake by first freshly grinding 1 to 2 oz. flax seed and blending it with 1½ cups pure water, 3 ice cubes and the juice of one freshly squeezed lemon. The flax will be fresher if you daily grind only the amount used for each shake. Be careful to avoid overblending which can overheat the flax seed and break down some of its essential oils and enzymes. A better recipe for the lemon-flax shake is use ESSIAC and flavonoid free radical scavenger herb tea (see recipe under herbs) instead of water and also add 1 oz. freshly ground milk thistle seed to neutralize free radicals and detoxify the liver.

Some people may be able to tolerate taking 1 to 2 tablespoons of fresh flax seed oil but many others with minor to severe liver and gall bladder problems may not. Using flax seed oil is not recommended in general and if it is used, take on an empty stomach first thing in the morning or in between meals to avoid coating the other foods in your stomach which causes indigestion, poor assimilation, constipation and toxicity.

Flax seed oil oxidizes extremely quickly and, as with all processed oils, should be sold in a refrigerated compartment, stamped with a short expiration date, packaged in a light-proof bottle, packed in nitrogen gas and preserved with natural d-alpha (not dl-alpha) vitamin E and herbal extracts of milk thistle and ginkgo. Otherwise, do not use flax seed oil in its free state. In any case, eating freshly ground flax seed is preferable to flax seed oil. Flax seedmeal (pre-ground flax seed) may be more convenient but freshly ground flax seed is much more fresh and better for you.

Flax seed is unique in containing a substance which resembles the prostaglandins known to regulate blood pressure and arterial function and have an important role in calcium and energy metabolism. Flax seed is rich in lecithin and phosphatides which aid in the digestion of oils and fats. It contains carotene and vitamin E. No other seed or food can match the benefits of flax seed.

Including ground flax seed and the EPA/GLA capsules (fish liver EPA oil with borage or primrose GLA oil) in your diet daily can significantly improve chronic constipation. At least once a week, my wife Roberleigh says, ''Thank you again for the EPA/GLA oil capsules because they give me the best bowel

movements that I have ever had.'' That always makes my day and
it sure is nice to have a sweet, pleasant wife and not some kind
of constipated, grumpy monster picking at you day and night. Not
that my wife was ever like that but if your spouse needs a
personality transplant, first try a little flax and fish liver oil to get
the bowels moving.

Again, rotate all foods to avoid allergy, Instead of eating flax
everyday, also rotate pumpkin, sunflower and sesame seeds in your
diet. Change fish liver oil brands every so often and switch back
and forth with borage and primrose oils.

Butter is better than margarine. Both are poor sources of essential fatty acids. Margarine is cheaper, contains less pesticides and
contains no antibiotics or cholesterol but it is harder to digest,
contains up to 60 percent cardiovascular and cancer causing trans
fatty acids, contains many non-natural chemicals used in the
hydrogenation process, easily denatured by heat, light and oxygen,
not good for frying and produces many very harmful free radicals,
a major, if not the most important, cause of disease.

Butter is more expensive, contains antibiotics, and contains
more pesticides but is easier to digest, contains 500 different
beneficial fatty acids, contains only 6 percent trans fatty acids,
tastes better and can be used for frying, baking and heating because
its saturated fats are more stable to heat, light and oxygen.

Butter does contain cholesterol and margarine does not but
the high trans fatty acids found in margarine and other altered oils
can increase blood cholesterol levels by 15 percent and triglyceride
levels by 47 percent very rapidly. Trans fatty acids increase the
size of atherosclerotic plaque and its effects are enhanced in the
presence of dietary cholesterol.

Trans fatty acid, not cholesterol, is the primary causative
factor. Yes, we should limit excess dietary cholesterol but it is
far more important and healthful to strictly limit trans fatty acids,
by totally eliminating margarine and other hydrogenated altered
oils.

In summary, butter is much better than margarine, especially
when it is raw and organic and free of pesticides and antibiotics.
Pasteurization is not necessary and it destroys many of the
beneficial qualities of natural butter. Unpasteurized raw butter is
actually more organic and chemical and germ-free than pasteurized
butter.

Butter, although better than margarine, is after all, a solid free oil with all the associated problems. Use a little butter sparingly but it is best to totally eliminate it when you are having indigestion or liver and gall bladder trouble.

Most people have chronic indigestion from eating free oils and fats, too much meat, overeating, etc. and they do not know it or they may pretend not to know. Perhaps you have had poor digestion and gastrointestinal problems so long that you think it is normal or, again, you may pretend to think it is normal. After your gastrointestinal tract cleans out, settles down and heals, you will feel better, have better digestion, assimilation and elimination and you will have less gastrointestinal distress.

And if you say that eating free oils does not cause any problems, chances are that you are not telling the truth, that your body is too numb and dead to feel pain or that you did not palpate the liver and gall bladder or examine yourself for symptoms properly. The point is that free oils cause health problems and you can find them if you look or have an alternative doctor help you look.

Your problem may be that you simply do not want to give up margarine, peanut butter, mayonnaise, salad dressing, lard, fatty meat, vegetable oils, fried foods, especially French fries, and all those other oils and fatty foods which taste so good and make you feel so energetic in the short run.

But once you have made the switch to a little butter, almond butter or natural non-hydrogenated peanut butter, cashew spread, salad dressing made from creamed whole seeds, nuts, avocado and olives, vegetables sauteed in liquid aminos or water and French fries made without oil, you will feel and look better. Eliminating free oils and fats and other unhealthful foods and bad habits from your diet will make you more healthy and some of your chronic diseases will start to improve.

OZONE OXYGEN THERAPY

Ozone is a form of oxygen and ozone therapy has been used for fifty years by thousands of German doctors who claim, in hundreds of scientific and clinical studies, that they are able to inactivate AIDS, Epstein-Barr, other viruses, candida, bacteria, fungi protozoa and cancer in diseased cells and actually enhance healthy cells as outlined in *Oxygen Therapies* by Ed McCabe and *Ozone in Medicine* by Dr. Gerard Sunnen, M.D. Anglo-American Research reports treating 35 AIDS patients successfully with ozone in three studies. In a German study, 576 AIDS patients of 690 were treated successfully with ozone therapy. McCabe and Sunnen say that ozone therapy has also been used successfully in the treatment of wound healing, burns, hepatitis, herpes, candidiasis, chronic fatigue syndrome, Alzheimers, Parkinson's, cancer, multiple sclerosis, arthritis, asthma, cardiovascular disease andother degenerative diseases.

Some of the medical Establishment's bad press on ozone therapy can be cleared up. Ozone has been likened to some foreign element floating around covering the globe or as a poison in smog. Actually, ozone is a natural product which by surrounding the planet, makes our lives possible, by filtering out burning rays. Ozone oxidizes pollutants in smog which makes it important to eliminate the pollutants, not the ozone. Medical ozone cannot cause an embolism when injected into the body. Ozone is not toxic and does not cause free radical pathology. On the contrary, ozone is converted in the body into hydroxyperoxides, a beneficial free radical scavenger, which superoxygenates the blood and tissues and destroys disease. German doctors have been using ozone for years with no side effects, report McCabe and Sunnen.

One type of medical ozone machine for around $2500 is used rectally or vaginally. Another type for approximately $5000 is used through the skin while inside a large bag something like a sleeping bag. The Food and Drug Administration has not approved treatment with ozone and routinely confiscates medical ozone machines from alternative medical doctors across America; therefore, patients and groups of patients combine their resources to purchase a machine and self-administer it.

Did you know that Los Angeles, Wiesbaden, Zurich, Florence, Marseille, Singapore, Moscow and other major cities use ozone to purify the city drinking water supplies? Ozone can be used to treat the water in your swimming pool and jacuzzi to replace the toxic chlorine presently used. Ozone machines are available to purify home drinking water. Air purification ozone machines ($500 approximately) effectively kill germs, viruses and molds in the air thereby decreasing colds, flu, infections, sinusitis and respiratory infections according to McCabe and Sunnen. Since ozone can be oxidative and irritating to the lungs and sinuses, the air purification machines are set low to produce just the right amount of ozone to prevent problems. Refer to the last chapter for more information about ozone machines.

Disclaimer: Information about ozone is for your education only and it is recommended that you consult an alternative medical doctor for the diagnosis and treatment of any health problem.

SALAD DRESSING

SALAD DRESSING — SEED

8 oz. water
8 oz. ground pumpkin or sunflower seeds
4 oz. toasted sesame seeds (half ground, half whole)
juice of 2 lemons or limes
2 tsp. herb seasoning (see Herbs for recipe)
½ tsp. sea salt
½ tsp. garlic powder
¼ tsp. cayenne powder

Blend all ingredients except sesame seeds until smooth. Add water if too thick or add more ground seeds if too thin. Taste test and add more seasoning if necessary. Add sesame seeds and stir. Use mechanically hulled sesame seeds. Unhulled sesame seeds tend to cause allergy.

Variation: Add 10 oz. silken tofu instead of water and perhaps just a little rice vinegar.

SALAD DRESSING — TOMATO

In a blender, blend:

> 15 oz. tomato sauce
> juice of 2 lemons or limes
> 1 or 2 tbsp. rice vinegar
> ½ to 1 tsp. garlic powder or fresh garlic
> ½ tsp. sea salt or to taste
> ¼ tsp. cayenne pepper

Stop blender and add ½ cup or more toasted sesame seeds (half whole, half ground) and blend briefly only to mix in the seeds. The toasted sesame seeds give a nice flavor and thicken the dressing. The more sesame seeds and the more you blend the dressing, the thicker it is. Taste test and add more seasoning to taste.

Variation: Use ground pumpkin or ground sunflower seeds instead of sesame or in addition to them. Another variation with tomato dressing is to add 10 oz. silken tofu and blend or add ginger sauce and stir it in to avoid breaking down the consistency of the ginger sauce.

SKIN PROBLEMS
MORE THAN SKIN DEEP

Topical applications of lotions and creams help skin problems but cleaning out the body, especially the bowels and liver, is more important. In *Food is Your Best Medicine*, the late Dr. Henry Bieler, M.D. states that when excess toxins from unhealthful foods and bad habits can no longer be adequately eliminated by the bowels, liver, urine and breath, these waste materials and poisons are forced out through the skin and also out through the vicarious pathways of the uterus, vagina, prostate and the female and male breasts and this is why we have an epidemic of skin, vaginal, uterine, prostate and breast cancer and health problems.

Skin problems indicate that your body, your bowels and your liver are filled to the brim and overflowing with toxins and no amount of cortisone, steroids, and antibiotics will cure the problem until you clean up your diet and lifestyle. Using underarm deodorants cannot cover up the odor for long because the stink is inside you just waiting to rise to the surface again and again.

Less than 10% of total daily calories in the right kind of essential oils and fats in your diet and the wrong kind of non-essential oils, such as polyunsaturated vegetable oils, oil salad dressings, pork and beef fat, mayonnaise, margarine, fried foods, chips and hydrogenated oils, cause skin problems and the right kind of oils, the essential oils found in fish, fish liver oil capsules, borage and primrose flower seed oil, and freshly ground flax, pumpkin, sunflower and sesame seeds, cure skin problems. The wrong kind of oils plug up and infect the skin's sebaceous glands and the good kind of oils clear them up.

Freshly ground flax seed added to cereal, grains, vegetables, applesauce and health shakes is specific treatment for acne. Also take a zinc supplement 30 mg daily. Give your children zinc tablets before, during and after puberty because the transition from childhood to adulthood depletes the body's zinc reserves which are involved in the production and function of sex hormones. Children and adults should eat lots of flax, pumpkin, sunflower and sesame seeds which are rich in zinc and, of course, the essential fatty acids. Eat seeds and nuts raw and whole but chew them well or they can be freshly ground or ground and creamed with water in a blender. See the recipes for seed milk.

A skin product called Hadapain made out of hydrogen peroxide and aloe can be applied topically to acne and other skiin problems, including staph infections. Note that staph infections can also be treated topically with grapefruit seed extract and orally with thymus gland extract. Topical applications of ozone also is a treatment for acne, staph and other skin infections. Order Hadapain, hydrogen peroxide and other oxygen products from The Family News, 777 S. State Rd., Suite 5-I, Margate, FL 33068, telephone (800) 284-6263.

To clean up the toxins inside your body and to clear up skin problems, eliminate the unhealthful foods, especially the wrong kind of oils, all dairy foods, sugar, white flour, white rice, white pasta, fried foods, chips and processed foods. Also eliminate the bad habits, smoking, alcohol, coffee, street drugs and medical drugs which slowly poison your body and your skin. Identify and treat any systemic toxicity, free radical pathology, candidiasis, allergy, parasites, hypothyroidism and other underlying metabolic disorders which toxify the body and skin.

Establishment dermatologists' understanding and treatment of skin disease is only skin deep. They treat only superficial skin symptoms with drugs and surgery. They apparently seem to have no problem recommending the unhealthful foods and oils or ignoring and minimizing the smoking, alcohol and other bad habits which cause skin problems. They tell you to stay out of the sun to avoid skin cancer but they do not tell you to correct the true cause of skin cancer, namely, systemic toxicity caused from unhealthful foods, bad habits and underlying metabolic disturbances.

The sun is not the primary cause of skin cancer. Skin cancer is caused by germs and viruses and lifestyle related toxins in the skin and sabeceous glands which interact with the sun and transform them into carcinogens. The key to prevent skin cancer and other skin problems is to improve the diet and habits, treat underlying metabolic disorders and clean up the accumulated toxins in the body, bowels, liver and skin.

TACOS

Sprout lentils. Cook regular or dextrinized brown rice.

Make a sauce by combining in a sauce pan:
    Salsa, drained well
    Ready Cut tomatoes, drained well
    tomato sauce
    garlic powder
    Italian herbs: oregano, basil, marjoram, rosemary,
      savory, garlic, sage
    a little lemon juice
    sea salt
Keep sauce as warm as possible without sticking.

Cut and chop the following vegetables and set aside in the refrigerator:
    Romaine lettuce
    red cabbage
    tomatoes
    green pepper
    celery
    sliced black ripe olives
    cilantro or parsley, minced
    carrots
    fresh corn or thawed frozen corn (do not cook)

Have available cayenne, onion and garlic powder, ground cumin and liquid aminos. Grind 1 cup raw pumpkin or sunflower seeds and set aside. You will also need salsa and cashew spread as condiments.

This recipe uses sprouted lentils. To sprout lentils, soak lentils in water in a container in the refrigerator overnight; discard water; place lentils in a large plastic collander; place a clean wet dish towel on top and wet down well; drain; place collander in a large bowl; wet down or fill bowl with water twice a day and drain well each time; should have sprouts in a couple of days; place in a bag and refrigerate until needed; can eat raw in salads or can saute, steam or boil them; sprouting adds many more nutrients and improves digestion. Cooked pinto beans or baked tofu can be substituted for the lentils.

Saute lots of sprouted lentils in an enameled iron or Vision skillet with garlic and onion powder, cayenne, ground cumin seeds, ground pumpkin or sunflower seeds, Italian herbs and liquid aminos; allow to cool or quick cool the sauteed lentils by placing them in a stainless steel bowl and put them in the freezer for a short time; when cool, mince the sauteed lentils with the bottom blade of a kitchen machine but do not make them pasty and sticky; place in the iron skillet, heat and keep warm.

Freshen taco shells by placing them in the racks of the oven at 425° F and keep checking them until crisp. Use aluminum foil on the bottom of the oven to catch the dripping oil. Place in a large bowl.

Mix the cooked rice and sauce together. Taste test and add more seasoning if necessary. Add the lentils and cut vegetables and mix together briefly. Taste test again and add seasoning if necessary. Place the filling in each taco shell and serve. Put a dish of salsa and cashew spread (substitute for cheese and sour cream) on the table for condiments.

TEMPEH

TEMPEH SANDWICHES ARE GREAT

Tempeh is a staple food of Indonesia. It is made from cooked soy beans with a live culture added which grows through the soy beans producing a high quality protein. You will find tempeh in health food stores and supermarkets in the frozen food section.

Ingredients for tempeh sandwiches:
        tempeh
        sliced whole wheat bread
        cole slaw
        sliced tomatoes
        horseradish sauce and mustard
        liquid aminos
        cayenne pepper
        cashew spread
        sliced sweet onions (optional)

To make tempeh sandwiches, place frozen tempeh in a baking pan and thaw and bake at 425°F for 20 minutes. Remove and cut into sandwich size and then slice in half to make thinner. Timing is important. After the tempeh is baked and sliced, make herb tea and get the bread out. Make a cole slaw from chopped cabbage, cashew cream and sea salt. Slice tomatoes and have herb seasoning, garlic powder, cayenne pepper and sea salt handy.

Heat up an enameled iron skillet on the high setting. Make a sauce from 4 tbsp. mustard, 1 tbsp. horseradish, lots of liquid aminos and a dash of cayenne pepper and garlic.

Place the tempeh slices in the buttered skillet. Spread the sauce on top and turn them over and cook just long enough to brown the sauce well. Use extra liquid aminos to moisten the tempeh. While browning, spread the top with sauce and turn over when the bottom side is browned. Be careful not to burn them. Place the browned tempeh on a plate and prepare the sandwiches.

Spread cashew spread on both slices of bread and put a little mustard/horseradish sauce on one of the slices. Next, put some cole slaw on top of one slice followed by tempeh and sliced tomato and optional sliced sweet onion. Add the seasoning (garlic powder, cayenne and herbal seasoning) and sprouts. Cut in half and serve. Delicious.

TEMPEH SAUTEED, WITH BROWN RICE OR MILLET

Cook brown rice or millet and add 1 cup cooked green peas. Chop 2 cups of tempeh into bite size pieces. Make a marinade sauce of liquid aminos, garlic powder and cayenne pepper. Preheat an enameled iron skillet on the high setting. Put a little butter in the skillet and saute the tempeh with the marinade sauce adding more liquid aminos or water if necessary.

Mix the cooked tempeh with the cooked rice or millet and cooked green peas and a little liquid aminos. If millet is used, stir very gently to avoid breaking it down. Serve with a salad and a steamed green vegetable.

TEMPEH VEGETABLE STEW

> tempeh
> 2 baked and chopped potatoes
> 2 stalks chopped celery
> 1 cup chopped cauliflower
> 1 chopped green pepper
> 2 sliced carrots
> 1 sliced zucchini
> 1 cup sliced mushrooms
> ½ tsp. garlic powder
> ¼ tsp. cayenne pepper
> ½ tsp. sea salt
> 1 bay leaf
> 1 or 2 tsp. herb seasoning
> or 1 tsp. oregano/¼ tsp. thyme
> ½ cup toasted sesame seeds
> ½ cup red wine
> 8 oz. tomato sauce
> juice of 1 lemon

Thaw and cut the tempeh into bite size pieces and saute with liquid aminos, garlic powder and cayenne pepper. Saute the vegetables briefly. Except for the tempeh, mix everything in a large pot with a little water and cook until done on the light side. Add the tempeh and stir. Serve over brown rice or add the cooked rice to the stew.

THAI SWEET AND SOUR VEGETABLES

> 4 cups mixed chopped vegetables — selections:
> bamboo shoot strips, sliced water chestnuts, tomato,
> bell pepper, French cut green beans, miniature
> corn, asparagus, zucchini, mushrooms, etc.

Sauce:

12 oz. tomato sauce	½ tsp garlic powder
2 tbsp. lemon or lime juice	¼ tsp. cayenne pepper
3 tbsp. honey	½ tsp. sea salt

Mix all of the sauce ingredients together and simmer. Add a little water if it gets too thick. The sauce should be on the thin side. Taste test and add more honey, lemon juice or other seasoning if necessary.

If string beans and other vegetables which require longer cooking are selected, cook them by themselves and add them to the others. Chop the remaining vegetables and place all of the vegetables in with sauce. Stir and simmer until done but do not overcook. When done, add one pat of butter for flavor. Garnish with cilantro or regular parsley and serve on top of brown rice or millet. Serve lemongrass tea. Variation: Add baked tofu.

THAI TOFU OR FISH WITH PEANUT BUTTER SAUCE

½ cup lemongrass herb
2 bay leaves
1 cup linden (lime) flower herb
1 cup freshly ground peanut butter — nothing added
  or almond butter
juice of lemon
1 cup coconut milk or unsweetened dried coconut
1 tsp. cinnamon
1 tsp. curry powder
½ tsp. garlic powder
2 tbsp. honey
tamarind sauce, if you can find it
Mahimahi or other white fish
toasted hulled sesame seeds
chopped red cabbage

Make a strong tea out of the lemongrass, linden flower and bay leaf herbs using 2 or 3 cups water; strain; discard used herbs; and pour 2 cups of the tea into a blender. Save the rest of the tea to thin out the sauce if necessary. Add all of the other ingredients and blend until smooth, adding just enough of the remaining herb tea or water to keep the blender going. Make it thick but thin enough to pour easily over the fish.

Place the fish in a buttered skillet, sprinkle on lemon juice, liquid aminos, garlic powder and cayenne pepper; bake at 425°F until done; cut into bite size pieces; and saute briefly with liquid aminos, garlic powder, cayenne and toasted hulled sesame seeds. Or use baked tofu — see recipe.

Chop red cabbage and place it on a plate; put the fish or tofu on top of the pile of cabbage; and pour the peanut butter sauce on top. Serve with brown rice, a cooked vegetable and lemongrass tea.

TOFU, BAKED

Preheat the oven to 425°F. Slice firm tofu into bite size pieces and sprinkle with garlic powder, cayenne pepper and herb seasoning and place in a buttered enameled iron skillet and bake at 425°F until browned and a little chewy in texture. After 20 minutes, check, remove any excess liquid, continue baking, turn over with a flat spatula, check every 10 minutes or so and continue until it is browned the way you like it. Remove from the oven, sprinkle and saute with liquid aminos and place in a covered dish until served with brown rice, millet or vegetables. Excellent with ginger sauce. For sandwiches, cut the tofu in larger thinner slices and bake as above.

TOXICITY AND CONSTIPATION

How your orthodox doctor keeps you toxic, constipated, sick and dependent and how you can eliminate these problems, including the doctor who has been deceiving you all these years.

"I have regular bowel movements. I don't need a laxative or a colonic," you might say. Maybe not but most Americans are constipated from underlying metabolic disorders, such as food allergy, hypothyroidism, candidiasis, hiatal hernia, low stomach acid and from a diet of dairy foods, free oils, sugar, sticky white flour bread and pasta, too much meat and not enough fiber and water.

What you may "think" and "believe" to be true about constipation may not be true at all because your doctors and nutritionists have misled you by telling you the following untruths: 1. Normal frequency of bowel movements varies from three times a day to once in three days. 2. Anyone who does not believe number 1 is obsessive-compulsive, meaning that he's crazy if he doesn't believe his doctor. 3. A routine internal examination of the colon usually reveals a "pink" and "healthy" colon in those health nuts who constantly complain about imaginary constipation and a layer of accumulated feces and mucus with the appearance of black plastic surrounding the colon wall. 4. The large intestine is largely impermeable thereby keeping so-called bowel toxins safe inside the colon and out of the blood and lymph. 5. Constipation, bowel and systemic toxicity are favorite theories of quacks and hypochondriacs.

The truth is you can have three bowel movements daily and still be constipated and anyone who has only one bowel movement in three days is kidding himself if he doesn't know he is an accident waiting to happen. An examination may show a "pink" and what appears as a "healthy" colon but that does not mean the colon is not filled with toxins. The large intestine, compromised by its own depressed immune system in the colon wall, is very permeable to toxins and germs as a result of leaky gut syndrome allowing disease causing toxins to readily pass through the colon wall into the blood and lymph throughout the body. Any discussion or treatment of constipation must include the concept of tissue constipation or systemic toxicity as a result of these freely circulating and accumulating blood and lymph toxins. Systemic toxicity, along with free radical pathology, is a basic cause of all disease, despite claims to the contrary by orthodox medical doctors.

So-called regular bowel movements in reality means that in some individuals a very limited amount of waste material is able to push its way through an inflamed, spastic colon or the center of an abnormal mass of accumulated feces and mucus in some cases hardened to a consistency of black concrete and plastic along the sides of the colon wall. The person is able to have one or several bowel movements daily; he therefore thinks he is not constipated but he is nonetheless.

Regardless of what your doctor has told you, constipation means the body is being poisoned by toxins in the colon. Unfortunately, in the great majority of people, the colon wall's immune system has been damaged by these toxins making it permeable and leaky to colon toxins.

The secretory IgA immunoglobulins of the immune system found in the mucous membranes of the gastrointestinal tract, sinuses, throat, bronchi, lungs, skin, vagina, etc. serve as a barrier to the external world. In the the case of the colon, the sIgA in the colon wall keeps germs, undigested food molecules and toxins from being absorbed into the blood and lymph.

In a healthy person, adequate numbers of sIgA form sIgA complexes to the antigens which produce an immunologic tolerance and aid in its neutralization in the liver. However, an unhealthy diet, poor digestion, constipation, candidiasis, food allergy and stress depletes the amount of sIgA making the colon wall more permeable and allowing feces, pathogenic organisms, xenogenic antibodies from dairy and meat, large fat molecules, proteins and poisons to readily pass unprotected through the colon wall, into the bloodstream and thereby into every cell, tissue and system in the body. This is why it is called systemic toxicity; it affects the whole body causing autoimmune and other degenerative diseases and problems from head to toe.

Despite the fact that some constipated people have an accumulated black plastic lining of feces and mucus along the colon wall and while others have pink unobstructed colon walls, both groups are constipated with excess toxic material in the colon as well as the small intestine and they both are absorbing abnormal germs and toxins through the walls of the small and large intestines making every cell and tissue in the whole body toxic and sick. The role of diet and good bowel elimination is clear in this.

Your constipated Establishment doctor recommends the standard "balanced" diet of too much fat, dairy, free oils, too much meat, the wrong kind of meat, pork, processed carbohydrates, too little fiber and spoiled foods passed off as fresh which cause indigestion, poor assimilation, constipation, systemic toxicity, free radical pathology and disease.

You may be unaware that the colon remains chronically impacted with accumulated feces and mucus backed all the way up to the small intestine causing the ileocecal valve to remain open abnormally. In this area, large amounts of mucus, especially from dairy foods and candidiasis, provide an ideal habitat for thousands or millions of intestinal parasites and pathogenic bacteria, which poison and damage the body and cause many diseases. In fact, it is called the region of worms. If the ileocecal valve is open when it should not be, parasites, worms, germs and toxins can spread up into the small intestine.

Parasites, worms and candida yeast germs embed themselves in the colon wall causing inflammatory and immunological responses and making the wall more permeable to other organisms, partially digested food, decomposed animal and plant material, macromolecules and toxins which then enter the bloodstream and lymph system.

Over 400 species of microflora inhabit the intestines; some are beneficial, like acidolphilus, and some are pathogenic. Pathogenic bacteria, yeast germs and viruses thrive in the intestines compromised by toxins from unhealthful foods and bad habits, too many starches and sugars, too little fiber and water, antibiotic therapy, an imbalance in the ratio of friendly to unfriendly bacteria and a depressed immune system in the intestinal wall.

The pathogenic organisms produce toxins, carcinogenic and tumor promoting substances, organic amines and cross-reactive antibodies which can initiate autoimmune and chronic inflammatory diseases, such as Crohn's disease, lupus, psoriasis, rheumatoid arthritis and other diseases.

When the intestines are unhealthy for all the reasons stated above, the pathogenic microflora reproduce out of control causing infection, toxicity, inflammation and disease, which spreads via the lymph and blood to the entire body. Klebsiella bacterial infection can cause kidney infection, septicemia blood infection and can produce harmful antigens and antibodies which can cause the body to attack itself, in what is known as autoimmune diseases, such as general joint and back stiffness and pain, rheumatoid arthritis, ankylosing spondylitis, myasthenia gravis, lupus, pernicious anemia, diabetes and other diseases.

Certain strains of E. coli bacteria can cause septicemia, high fever, diabetes mellitus, bacterial meningitis, myasthenia gravis and other diseases. Yersinia enterocolitica bacteria can cause thyroiditis. Anaerobic bacteria can cause ulcerative colitis. The list goes on and on.

The unhealthy colon is therefore a breeding ground for bacterial and viral disease and systemic toxicity which affect the whole body.

The elimininative organs cannot possibly effectively eliminate all the toxins from a constant input of unhealthful foods, bad habits (smoking, alcohol, coffee, soft drinks, street drugs, medical drugs, etc.), environmental pollutants and untreated underlying metabolic disorders (allergy, candidiasis, parasites, pathogenic bacteria, hypothyroidism, etc.). The bloodstream becomes increasingly filled to overflowing with disease organisms, protein parts from dead candida and other organisms, macromolecules of food, food proteins and toxins where they circulate around the body causing inflammation, water retention, weight gain, irritation, corrosion, damage and disease.

Feces and toxins abnormally recirculated in the bloodstream as a result of chronic constipation explains why the eliminative organs of the skin and lungs have a strangely familiar unpleasant odor. Intestinal toxins in the bloodstream exiting through the skin and lungs ooze out of the skin in the form of smelly sweat and out of the lungs in the form of bad breath that smells like feces. Toxic bowels and impure blood also cause excess sweating and skin problems, including skin cancer. We all sweat and breathe but there is no good reason why our bodies and breath should not smell sweet. Underarm deodorant and breath mints help but the real solution lies in cleaning up your colon and your diet.

As a protective measure to get the disease-causing toxins out of circulation, the body removes diet-related and metabolic poisons from the bloodstream and lymph and deposits and stores them in cells and tissues, out of the way, so to speak, as long as the person is taking in that particular offending unhealthful food, allergen, bad habit, smoking, alcohol, coffee, drugs, etc. When you stop eating unhealthful foods, especially the ones which you have become allergic or addicted to or when you eliminate those cigarettes, coffee, medical drugs, street drugs and alcohol, all those stored cell and tissue toxins are suddenly dumped into the bloodstream on their way out of the body irritating your nervous system and appetite control centers.

The toxic release is what causes your fatigue, jumpy nerves, strong appetite, bad moods, etc. You crave and seek out the unhealthful food or bad habit which will stop the release of toxins and make you feel better but only temporarily. Soon you almost automatically reach out for a dairy food or a cigarette, for example, to ward off the withdrawal symptoms.

This aggravation or worsening of symptoms is called a healing crisis. The person detoxifying from a toxin may get worse before he gets better and he tends to crave the very food or habit which made him toxic initially.

As soon as the person ingests a toxin from a food or smoking, alcohol, drugs, coffee, or some other bad habit, the cells stop eliminating that particular toxin and start accumulating it again in an effort to keep the toxin out of blood circulation to minimize damage and to decrease any craving or other symptoms of that toxin. The person consequently feels better after he gets his fix but he soon feels worse when his cells again start dumping the toxins and it's time for another fix and so on in a vicious pattern of underlying toxicity, allergy and addiction and all the hundreds of unnecessary illnesses and diseases they cause, if ignored, misdiagnosed and left untreated by orthodox doctors.

Disease starts in the colon. Colon toxins spread via the bloodstream and lymph system to all tissues causing inflammation, irritation, edema, swelling, congestion, damage and disease in ways that are difficult to recognize or understand. Colon toxicity and undigested wheat gluten residues, for example, buildup in the colon aggravate or cause low back, sacroiliac, hip, knee and leg problems, sex organ problems, hayfever, rashes, sore throat, neck problems, excess sweating, gas, more constipation, flu, colds, skin disorders, bad breath, low resistance, allergy and all the typical health problems wrongfully attributed to germs and so-called chemical imbalances. Chronic colon and tissue constipation also causes arthritis, cancer, candidiasis and other degenerative diseases. You may not want to believe it but it is true. Systemic toxicity, free radical pathology, constipation, candidiasis and other underlying metabolic diseases are, in fact, the most important theories of disease and health. Your toxic colon makes you sick by poisoning your whole body and destroying your immune system making you more susceptible to all sorts of health problems. Your nerves, muscles, joints and metabolic system cannot operate smoothly and efficiently when constantly poisoned, inflamed, irritated and damaged by tissue toxins.

Systemic toxicity and inflammation causes the body to retain water causing edema, swelling, spongy untoned tissue, pain and weight gain. Water is retained in the body as a defense mechanism to weaken the solution of toxins in the tissues. When you detoxify the body and stop unhealthful foods and bad habits which poison the body, systemic toxicity and inflammation are decreased and you lose pounds of water weight because your body does not need the water to neutralize and protect the body. But when you poison the body again with unhealthful foods and bad habits, you are likely to regain the water weight and be back where you started, toxic, sick and overweight.

Treatment for an unhealthy colon, constipation and systemic toxicity and all the thousands of symptoms and diseases they cause can begin with an examination by an alternative doctor (medical doctor, nutritional chiropractor or naturopath). The alternative doctor will take a complete history, examine the patient's body with his hands to locate sensitivity, inflammation, edema, swelling, congestion, pain and stiffness.

Systemic toxicity can be diagnosed by: white tongue, excessive thirst, mouth hanging open, puffiness, swelling, edema, eye bags, dark circles under the eyes, lifeless eyes, obesity, fatigue, allergy, depression, sleep disturbances, rapid or irregular heartbeat, constipation, inadequate water intake, skin problems, frequent or severe colds, flu and infection, prolonged illness, chronic disease, failed treatment, general stiffness and pain in joints, neck, back and feet, sensitive reflex points on bottom of feet, use of alcohol, street drugs, medical drugs, coffee, junk foods, etc.

A hands on, palpation examination by an experienced alternative doctor will find evidence of systemic toxicity manifesting as inflammation, warmth, coldness, swelling, edema, sensitivity, pain, congestion, crystals, spasms, stiffness, hardness, etc. directly on or near the eliminative organs, which are being overworked, exhausted and damaged by daily abuse from unhealthful foods and bad habits and untreated metabolic disorders.

Palpation of the eliminative organs turns up the above evidence of dysfunction, sub-clinical and clinical disease in the following locations: lung toxicity — spinous tip (center) pain of T4 to T6 vertebrae indicating irritation of spinal nerves to lungs; liver-gall bladder toxicity — reflex pain in shoulders and between spine and right shoulder blade and direct pain over liver and gall bladder; kidney toxicity — transverse spinous process (sides) of T10 to L2 vertebrae and psoas-iliacus muscle spasm and pain in the groin and waist; small and large intestine toxicity — sensitivity and pain directly on the small and large intestine; sinus cavity toxicity — inflammation, sensitivity, and pain directly on or near the sinuses; lymph node toxicity — inflammation, swelling, congestion, sensitivity and pain directly on lymph nodes and a general achiness in the area; whole body toxicity — indicated by inflammation, swelling, edema, stiffness, aches and pain almost everywhere on the body.

The average person tends to be defensive and not likely to admit to having pain and health problems related to unhealthful foods and bad habits, which they do not want to give up. Typically, a toxic person will say that he is: healthy; does not have any problems or pain; favorite unhealthful foods and bad habits do not affect him; etc. However, a good history and a good palpation examination will show otherwise, namely, pain associated with toxic, worn out eliminative organs, visual evidence (eye bags, edema, obesity, etc.) of systemic toxicity, and sometimes sensitivity and pain every place the body is deeply palpated.

The average toxic, sick person suffering from his own self-inflicted unhealthful lifestyle will usually defend himself with such lame excuses as, ''I didn't know that I had pain there!'' or, ''If you (the doctor) would stop poking me so hard, it wouldn't hurt!'' when in fact, he secretly suffers discomfort, stiffness and pain daily but is too stubborn to admit it, even when he pays an alternative doctor to give him health advice.

Some patients are so toxic and so sick that their suffering, miserable pain-filled, toxic, sick bodies have turned off the pain as a defense measure meaning they cannot feel the pain. Usually, after two or three sessions of deep bodywork and chiropractic adjustments, the affected area wakes up allowing the person to feel the pain which was previously blocked by chronicity over a period of time.

The average person, therefore, goes to orthodox medical doctors who let him get away with his unhealthful lifestyle and avoids alternative doctors who consider it their professional duty to skillfully and lovingly (and sometimes not so skillfully and not so lovingly) confront the patient to improve his diet and give up his bad habits.

A good diagnosis of systemic toxicity, constipation and *ANY* difficult health problem resistant to diagnosis and effective treatment should include a Comprehensive Stool and Digestive Analysis from a laboratory associated with alternative medical doctors. I recommend the Meridan Valley Clinical Laboratory, 24030 132nd Avenue, SE, Kent, WA 98042, telephone (800) 234-6825 or (206) 631-8922 associated with Dr. Jonathan Wright, M.D., a well known alternative medical doctor. Lab kits are delivered and picked up by an overnight carrier anywhere in the United States, including Hawaii and Alaska.

The Comprehensive Stool and Digestive Analysis evaluates: digestion and assimilation of fat, carbohydrate and protein; food and environmental allergy; hypochlorhydria, pancreatic insufficiency, malabsorption, occult blood, parasites, ova, pathogenic bacteria, candida, colon cancer risk, chronic intestinal complaints, intestinal inflammation, intestinal hypermotility, irritable bowel, spastic colon, indigestion, bloating, gas, etc. Again, this one inexpensive lab test could possibly point to a more definitive diagnosis and more effective treatment for those health problems which are hard to diagnose and treat.

In consideration that most diagnostic tests are unnecessary, inaccurate, wasteful, a symptom of defensive medicine and part of a scheme to make money at your expense, an ethical doctor would give you this lab test first before wasting thousands of your dollars on less productive diagnostics.

Food allergy testing is also critically important in that most toxicity, most free radical pathology and most health problems are caused by food allergy. Follow the food allergy testing program in chapter one or contact the American Association of Acupuncture and Bio-Energetic Medicine in the last chapter for a referral to an alternative doctor who uses the Computron, Interro or Listen electrodiagnosis for allergy and health problems.

After all the results are in and you have a good diagnosis of what is making you toxic and sick, treatment should include: gradually or slowly eliminating the unhealthful foods and bad habits to zero because your body will continue to accumulate a particular toxin or allergen until you completely stop the source of the toxin or allergy and then your body will start to heal much more effectively; treating special metabolic disorders (i.e., food allergy, hypochlorhydria, hypothyroidism, hiatal hernia, etc.) with natural therapies; taking acidolphilus to replace friendly bacteria if antibiotic therapy is necessary; resting; exercise; and step one, of course, to get your heart and spirit ready for healing and wellness.

When you take steps to neutralize the toxins in the bloodstream and colon as they are being released, you may be more successful in living through the withdrawal pains from giving up your favorite poisons. Eat a temporary alkaline diet for only one to three days of only cooked root and green leafy vegetables to help de-acidify and detoxify the acidic toxins in your body. In addition to an herbal laxative, take one enema or colonic a day for 7 days, if your doctor and you determine that it is safe to do so. Then take one per week and repeat the 7 day cleansing program every 6 weeks as long as you need to. A good colon cleansing program will help neutralize and eliminate toxins released by the withdrawal and detoxification process.

Eliminate dairy which is one of the most mucus forming and constipating foods you can eat. Drink 2 to 3 quarts of pure water a day. Eat more fiber rich foods. Stop eating free oils and fats which increase your normal 24 hour transit time of ingested foods from mouth to anus to 80 to 100 hours.

A clean colon and a clean body mean that chronic constipation and systemic toxicity will no longer cause inflammatory responses, edema, pain, degeneration and disease in your body. Your injuries may heal for the first time, your muscles will tone up and any water retention will melt away to help you shed extra pounds.

Your healthier colon will growl and talk to you and will tell you right away when you eat the wrong foods. You will have taken a major step toward rejuvenating your whole body, mind and spirit and you will have a new sparkle in your eye not to mention your colon.

VEGETABLES

VEGETABLES: GINGER SAUCE
SWEET AND SOUR VEGETABLES

2 cups chopped ginger
36 oz. frozen apple juice concentrate
1 cup raw honey
juice of 3 lemons
10 heaping tbsp. arrowroot powder

2 large chopped eggplant;
3 thinly sliced carrots
1 tub firm tofu
1 chopped zucchini
3 chopped green pepper
5 sliced mushrooms

Preheat the oven to 425°F and preheat and boil a 5 quart pot half filled with water using the high setting. The eggplant and tofu are baked so start with them first. Slice and cut the eggplant into bite size pieces, sprinkle with herb seasoning, garlic powder, cayenne pepper and Bragg's Liquid Aminos, place in a large buttered baking pan and bake in the oven. Prepare the tofu in the same manner with the same seasoning, place in a separate buttered baking pan and bake. Set the timer for 20 minutes for both the eggplant and the tofu. Remove the eggplant after 20 minutes, pour in enough water to cover the bottom, turn over with a flat spatula, bake for another 20 minutes and continue baking until done. Approximate baking time 1 hour for the eggplant.

Likewise, with the tofu, remove after 20 minutes. Remove any excess liquid, turn over and continue baking until golden brown which may take around 45 minutes. When done, sprinkle with liquid aminos and place in a covered dish. Cover the eggplant with the tofu when it is ready.

Chop the green pepper and zucchini and slice the carrots and mushrooms and chill until later.

Check on the water in the pot to make sure it is getting as hot as possible. Mince the ginger with the bottom blade of the Cuisinart or kitchen machine and blend at high speed in a Vita Mix or blender with half of the apple juice concentrate (no water added). blend until smooth and then add the honey, lemon juice, arrowroot and the rest of the apple juice concentrate. When the water is boiling or as hot as possible, pour in all the blended ingredients and stir constantly with a flat spatula. It should thicken right away if the water is hot enough. Fill the water up to the top, stir and taste test and add more honey or lemon juice to your own taste.

To serve, warm up the eggplant and tofu and add it to the raw green pepper, zucchini, carrot and mushrooms in a large mixing bowl. No need to cook them. Mix the vegetables and add just enough ginger sauce to suit your taste. Serve over brown rice and place a server full of ginger sauce on the table. Store excess in the refrigerator and it will last around 2 weeks. Keep a ready supply of ginger sauce to add to grains, salad dressing and other recipes and your friends will beg for it.

VEGETABLES: GRADY'S PATE

> 1 cup dextrinized brown rice
> 1 cup sprouted and cooked lentils
>
> 2 green peppers
> 6 carrots
> 6 stalks celery
> 2 cups corn kernels
>
> 1 cup cashews
> 1 cup pumpkin seeds
> 1 cup toasted sesame seeds
>
> ½ cup unpasteurized miso (mix half unpasteurized
>   dark miso and unpasteurized light miso)
> 2 tbsp. vegetable broth powder
> 2 tsp. garlic powder or fresh garlic
> ½ tsp. cayenne pepper
> 2 tbsp. Bronner's Mineral Bouillon, or
>   Bragg's Liquid Aminos or   (cont. next page)

soy sauce — use more to taste
salt to taste

Pre-toast the brown rice and cook to dextrinize it. Sprout the lentils, steam briefly and then saute in Bragg's Liquid Aminos or soy sauce along with garlic powder. Set aside to allow rice and lentils to cool. Note that raw instead of cooked lentil sprouts seems like a good idea but the raw sprouts leave a sharp, raw taste. Steam and saute them just enough to make them taste better.

Place raw vegetables in a kitchen machine using the bottom blade and mince fine. Take a straining cloth (washed new cotton baby diaper) and place it over a large bowl; place the minced vegetables in the middle of the baby diaper, bring the diaper corners together and twist the minced vegetables to drain the liquid (drink the vegetable juice); and place the drained vegetables aside in a small bowl.

Grind the nuts and seeds in a coffee grinder.

Place the cooked rice and lentils in a kitchen machine using the bottom blade and make a smooth paste — it takes some time so be patient. Add the remaining ingredients including spices in the kitchen machine with the rice and lentils and make a smooth paste. Taste test and add more bouillon, seasoning, etc. to taste. Refrigerate and serve in a bowl. Toast plain corn tortillas (corn, water, lime only — no oil) in the oven to make them crisp. Cut up some carrot, celery and green pepper sticks. Serve pate with toasted corn tortillas and vegetable sticks.

WEIGHT LOSS PERMANENTLY

Two-thirds of the adult population and about one-third of children are overweight or obese in the United States. No one likes to have weight problems, yet only 66% of overweight people and only 5% of obese people are able to attain and maintain normal body weight and as you may know, fat children are likely to be fat adults.

Why are Americans so fat? It becomes crystal clear to alternative doctors but not to orthodox doctors that overweight and obese people are sick; that weight problems are a symptom of their sickness; that Establishment doctors recommend the wrong foods and the wrong weight loss diets; that orthodox medical doctors ignore, minimize, misdiagnose and mistreat the hypothyroidism, food allergy, systemic toxicity, free radical pathology, candidiasis, hiatal hernia, hypoglycemia, diabetes and other underlying metabolic disorders which make you sick and fat; and that the processed food industry, the media, the "health" charities and the government "health" agencies and courts, and the $800 billion a year medical Establishment get richer and more powerful making you ill, overweight and more dependent upon Big Brother.

The low calorie or high protein weight loss diets long touted by the medical monopoly, the processed food industry and the Establishment media emphasizing lean meat, poultry, fish, low fat milk and cheese, vegetables, fruit and protein drinks made from processed milk and egg products don't work except in the short run when you lose weight at first only to gain it back within a year.

These Establishment quick weight loss diets are not effective as we all know. Quick weight loss is an appealing idea but *PERMANENT WEIGHT LOSS* is a better idea but not so appealing unless you are willing to work a little harder to develop a wellness lifestyle. Low calories sounds good but diets that severely restrict caloric intake and prolonged fasting are scientifically undesirable, make you lose lean muscle not fat and can be medically dangerous by causing gallstones, impaired glucose intolerance, high blood serum levels of uric acid with decreased urinary output, loss of electrolytes, calcium, potassium, sodium, magnesium and phosphate, reductions in blood volume and body fluids, congestive heart failure and sudden death.

You can lose weight fast on the high protein diet and it prevents loss of lean muscle but unfortunately causes systemic toxicity and kidney damage and gives the false impression that your body can handle all that protein when it cannot — far from it.

All of the quick weight loss diets include unhealthful, allergenic, processed foods, such as milk, whey, soy and egg solids, which sooner or later cause water retention, metabolic dysfunction and weight gain. You cannot lose weight permanently until you eliminate all milk, whey, cheese, sourcream, yogurt and ice cream from your diet and you can begin to understand this when you read the chapter on dairy foods. Fresh organic eggs and natural soy products are a good food once or twice a week but if you try to eat them every day over a period of months on some type of quick weight loss diet, especially when they are overprocessed in the form of protein drinks, you are likely to become allergic and toxic to them. They may make you sick and you may not lose much weight.

Quick weight loss diets typically contain little or no oils and fats and if they are allowed on the diet at all, they are usually the wrong kind, i.e., margarine, vegetable oil, no essential fatty acids, etc. Take another look at the chapter on oils and fats. Linolenic and linoleic essential fatty acids are "essential" not optional nutrients your body needs every day to stay healthy at the cellular level and when your weight loss and regular diets do not contain them, you may develop health problems and your orthodox doctor is not likely to have a clue why.

When you hear about people getting sick on the fad diets, now you will know that the lack of essential fatty acids is a major cause. The average person eats way too many oils and fats, around 50% of total calories, but too little also causes problems in that less than 10% of your daily calories in oils and fats causes cancer and other degenerative diseases. This is why it is important to eat 15% of your daily calories in the essential fatty acid foods, fish, fish oil capsules and flax, pumpkin, sunflower and sesame seeds. Note that essential oils actually speed up metabolism and weight loss.

In review, orthodox quick weight loss diets recommend the wrong foods. You lose a little weight, mostly good, lean muscle but you gain it back in the form of more fat cells. You learn little or absolutely nothing about your body, its metabolic functions, its requirements and what to do when it falls apart. And when your diet is finished or when it finishes you, your orthodox doctor or nutritionist is likely to recommend a "balanced" diet of more of the wrong foods which may make you more imbalanced, needy, ravenous and emotionally crippled and it may take you months, years or a lifetime to recover your vitality and health.

The majority of overweight people are suffering from hypothyroidism, food allergy, toxicity, hypoglycemia, borderline diabetes and most of the other underlying metabolic disorders which are routinely mismanaged by orthodox medical doctors but treated effectively by alternative doctors. This means that if you want to lose weight and keep it off, you may need to see an alternative doctor to help you test and treat underlying metabolic disorders which may prevent weight loss.

In brief, clinical and even borderline sub-clinical hypothyroidism in about half the population and thyroiditis in approximately 2% of the population are major causes of sickness and weight problems. Low or impaired thyroid function upsets all of your body's physiological metabolic processes in all of your organs and glands creating havoc in the digestion and assimilation of foods and the elimination of waste. Enzymes, hormones and bio-chemicals work in your body to keep you healthy and slim only within a very narrow temperature range and if a thyroid problem keeps your body temperature below normal, how can your life functions be normal? Hypothyroidism and thyroiditis cause the adrenal glands, the liver and gall bladder, the pancreas, the stomach, the intestines, the blood circulation and the brain and nervous system to slow down. No wonder you gain weight and suffer from the fatigue, depression, constipation, stiffness, pain and poor memory associated with thyroid dysfunction.

Carbohydrate intolerance, hypoglycemia and diabetes are also caused by hypothyroidism according to Dr. William Philpott, M.D., an alternative doctor. Too much sugar, sweets, white flour and processed carbohydrates, including alcohol — all pushed by the controlled media, stimulates the pancreas to produce too much insulin which causes the blood sugar to peak rapidly and then fall suddenly making you feel great one minute and then miserable and hungry the next, and this is known as hypoglycemia which your orthodox doctor does not take seriously. Soon your pancreas and related organs are worn out and exhausted and no longer able to produce enough insulin causing you to have too much sugar in your blood and urine runoff and this is your diabetes, for which your Establishment doctor gives you insulin but does not effectively treat the underlying hypothyroidism and the unhealthful diet which caused hypoglycemia, the diabetes and the weight gain. Both systemic toxicity from unhealthful foods, bad habits, candidiasis and food allergy from the wrong foods and overeating the same foods poison the entire body creating free radical pathology and causing congestion, inflammation, water retention, swelling, edema, constipation, muscle soreness, joint stiffness and pain, indigestion, poor assimilation, depression, arthritis, cardiovascular disease, cancer and other health problems. Consequently, you blow up like a balloon with all the water your tissues retain to water down and neutralize the toxins in your system; you are always hungry because you don't get much nutrition from the foods you eat; you get poisoned from all the candida toxins in your colon and body; you accumulate many pounds of feces and mucus in your constipated large intestine; your fat cells fill up with toxins; you crave the foods you are allergic to; you look and feel just terrible; and of course, all this means you gain weight and have a tendency to give up hope and eat everything in sight. But ask an orthodox doctor about the free radicals, symptoms and overweight and he is likely to think you have gone 'round the bend.

Your orthodox doctor may try to convince you that all these underlying metabolic disorders are not important causes of your weight problem and he "proves" it with a few simple lab tests, which always seem to report no problem when, in fact, you may have a serious problem, which he chooses to overlook or minimize.

If his drugs and diet pills don't seem to help you feel better or help you lose weight, he may blame you instead of himself and implies that all your health and weight problems are in your head. Out comes the psychiatric couch and the mind and mood drugs, which may make you worse.

What can you do to lose weight, keep it off and feel good about yourself? Find a good alternative medical doctor, nutritional chiropractor or naturopath and follow a program of natural foods and natural ways to lose weight to keep it off permanently.

1. Step One outlined in the chapter on Healing the Whole Person, Body, Mind and Spirit is a place to slim down and begin your new lifestyle. Release your problems, disappointments,

abandonment, rejection, victimizing behaviors, unhealthful foods, bad habits, poor self-concept and your resistance to losing those extra pounds to God; start loving yourself more; make a decision to get on the road to health and wellness; do it when you are ready and in the meantime, meditate, pray and believe you are worth it to try again and again.

2. Ask the alternative medical doctor, nutritional chiropractor or naturopath to help you diagnose and treat any underlying metabolic disorders which must be identified and corrected in order to lose weight effectively. Untreated metabolic disorders, such as hypothyroidism, food allergy, candidiasis, etc., are a primary cause of illness, disease and weight gain. Don't eat the same foods every day and as best as possible, rotate your foods every five days to avoid food allergy and weight problems.

3. Eat good, natural Detox Diet foods on a sensible weight loss program and as a permanent way to eat and live. Drink two to three quarts of filtered or distilled water a day. Raw fruits, vegetables and juices for breakfast and lunch cleanse the body daily and cooked grains with sprouted lentils, beans, tofu or tempeh and lightly steamed vegetables along with oil free salads and some raw seeds and nuts for dinner also cleanse the body and build it up, especially when you eat fish or eggs once or twice a week. You will not crave the wrong foods because you will feel nourished and your appetite will be satisfied. You will lose weight.

4. Eliminate the unhealthful processed foods, especially all sugar, white flour, sweets, dairy and the wrong kind of proteins, oils and fats, and eliminate the cigarettes, alcohol, coffee, street drugs, medical drugs and other bad habits which make you toxic, sick and overweight.

5. Substitute healthful foods and good habits. Try Grady's vegetable pate instead of liverwurst; experience his baked tofu instead of fried chicken; cashew spread instead of mayonnaise or sourcream; Rice Dream instead of ice cream; walnut gravy instead of regular meat gravy; Thai food instead of the same old tired foods; sweets made out of honey and date sugar instead of white sugar. When you go out for Mexican or Italian food, leave off the cheese or try tofu cheese. You get the idea.

6. Set your mind to a long term weight loss program to lose about two pounds a week and you will keep the weight off when you eliminate the dairy, free oils, sugar, excess protein, junk foods

and alcohol. In this way, you will lose fat, not lean muscle.

7. Limit quick weight loss diets to two weeks or four weeks and stick to the long term weight loss program after that. Prolonged fasting and diets that severely restrict caloric intake eat away your good lean muscle and replace it with fat.

8. With proper supervision, enjoy a fast for two to five days with lots of water and fresh vegetable juices, some fruit juice and whole fruit, herb tea and supplements or do a modified fast for two weeks with all of the above plus cooked vegetables, fresh vegetable salads and clean fish once or twice a week.

9. During a long term weight loss program or after two weeks of a quick weight loss program be sure to take 2 fish liver oil capsules with borage or primrose oil before lunch and dinner to provide the good kind of oils, linolenic, linoleic and gamma-linolenic (GLA) to provide both omega 3 and 6 essential fatty acids necessary to provide structural components of the cell membranes, lubricate the intestines for regular elimination, make your skin healthy, prevent blood platelet sticking and arteriosclerosis, bring oxygen into the system, stimulate metabolism, increase the metabolic rate and burn off excess fat and glucose. GLA reduces the appetite, activates enzyme systems that keep potassium and sodium in proper ratio in each cell, helps eliminate fat and inhibits transformation of carbohydrates into fat. Eliminate the wrong kind of oils and take in at least 15% of your calories in essential oils found in fresh fish, fish and borage and primrose oil capsules and fresh flax, sunflower, pumpkin and sesame seeds.

10. Take the following supplements during a 14 or 28 day quick weight loss program: a good mineral supplement with pancreatic enzymes before meals and if low stomach acid, take hydrochloric acid tablets after meals; 5 to 10 g vitamin C; and an herbal laxative and an enema or colonic every day or every other day. Take lipotropic agents (choline, inositol, taurine, dl methionine, black radish, green beet leaf, magnesium, celandine, raw liver concentrate, B6, folic acid, B12) and herbal cholagogues and choleretics, such as silymarin and dandelion root, to support liver function to help detoxify the whole body and lose weight. Carnitine can speed the burning of fat. Chromium GTF and/or picolinate can improve glucose toleraance, increase tissue sensitivity to insulin, normalize blood lipids, increase lean muscle, reduce cravings for sweets and aid in weight loss. Glucomannan and guar

gum capsules swell up after ingestion and may help decrease the appetite and help dieters to stay on a weight loss program. Use any of the above as needed on long term weight reduction programs.

11. Exercise to keep your body moving and losing weight, don't skip meals, get plenty of sleep and rest and stay active to fight off boredom. An endurance aerobic exercise program is recommended four days a week during a long term weight loss program and exercise daily on a two week quick weight loss diet, 20 to 30 minutes in duration at a minimum intensity of 60% heart rate and it is best to check with your alternative medical doctor first. Walking, swimming aquacise, water walking, yoga, stretching, breathing exercises, tai ·chi, martial arts, exercise machines, mini-trampoline, running and jogging will keep you fit and slim.

Begin your weight loss program by thinking thin. Make positive affirmations of thinness and visualize yourself thin. Create a strong clear desire to lose weight. Make a commitment to yourself. Reward yourself with an occasional natural treat, buy something or do something special. You will lose weight, love yourself more, feel better and have more energy and motivation. Remember that a clean, natural diet and healthy lifestyle makes you clean and slim.

WELLNESS DOCTOR REFERRALS AND RECOMMENDED READING

A Wellness Doctor's first concern is YOU, body, mind and spirit. He will try his best to see you promptly by not overbooking his schedule. He will spend time with you to discuss your problem. He will take a good history and palpate your body with his hands to detect problem areas and use all available information to diagnose you. He will use a few good laboratory tests, such as a comprehensive digestive and stool analysis, which can tell you a lot about any problems with digestion, low stomach acid, low pancreatic enzymes, liver and gall bladder problems, allergy, natural flora and any bacterial, viral or parasitic infections. He will use homeopathy, herbs, vitamins, minerals, enzymes, acupuncture, massage, chiropractic adjustments and he will treat underlying metabolic disorders, like hypothyroidism, to correct the cause of health problems not merely cover up their symptoms. If antibiotics are absolutely necessary, he will always prescribe acidolphilus to build up the natural immune protective flora to prevent candida overgrowth. He will use intravenous chelation, ozone therapy and other natural therapies proven effective in the treatment of cancer, cardiovascular disease, arthritis and other degenerative diseases. He will not overcharge you in that natural therapies are relatively inexpensive. He will teach you how to look at yourself with more honesty, how to eat healthful foods, how to substitute bad habits with good habits and how to live a wellness lifestyle.

All referrals are made to wellness oriented metabolic medical doctors, alternative osteopaths, nutritional chiropractors and naturopaths. The term metabolic refers to all the chemical and physiological metabolic processes by which the body digests, assimilates and eliminates food, minerals, vitamins and enzymes and converts it into energy, building units, living tissue and waste material. Metabolic is used as a code word to identify WELLNESS and nutritionally oriented doctors who use natural therapies to facilitate and improve natural metabolic functions of the body to eliminate the basic underlying causes of disease to set themselves apart from the drug oriented orthodox doctors who use toxic drugs to block or stimulate metabolic processes to relieve only superficial symptoms, which return again and again in various forms.

A short history of the politics of medicine will help you understand why it is so important to consult alternative medical doctors, nutritional chiropractors and naturopaths. By 1910, John D. Rockefeller had taken total control over the entire medical profession as documented in *Murder By Injection* by Eustace Mullins and *World Without Cancer* by G. Edward Griffin and make no mistake, the Rockefeller interests control modern medicine today.

Rockefeller set up the counterfeit ''humanitarian'' Rockefeller Foundation and the Rockefeller Institute of Medical Research and also dominated the Carnegie Foundation not to serve humanity but to enrich Rockefeller.

Griffin states, ''The American Medical Association climbed into bed with the Rockefeller and Carnegie interests in 1908 . . . The end result was that all medical schools became heavily oriented toward drugs and drug research, for it was through the increased sale of these drugs'' that Rockefeller realized a profit on his investment. Now the Rockefeller medical Establishment rakes in $800 billion a year. Are we better off? No, the once great United States is one of the sickest nations in the world thanks to Rockefeller.

Rockefeller owns most of the petroleum industry and the medical drug and vaccine industry which uses petroleum products in the manufacture of the drugs and he also owns most of the processed and junk food industry. The Rockefeller scheme was simple and massive: bribe the medical schools and associations through his bogus philanthropic foundations with millions of dollars not for natural therapies but only for Rockefeller drug research to influence the medical Establishment to push Rockefeller toxic petro-chemical drugs and recommend Rockefeller toxic petrochemical processed and junk foods to pay back his bribes.

Rockefeller consolidated his control by establishing a medical monopoly in short order by eliminating all competition to the drug approach. He did this through his agents, bureaucrats, politicians and media propagandists who fabricated false reports, much like today, against alternative doctors and natural therapies like chelation and ozone.

In the early 1900s, fully two-thirds of all medical doctors were homeopaths dedicated to research and treatment using vitamins, minerals, enzymes, herbs and other natural therapies. Rockefeller paid off his agents to discredit and outlaw all homeopathic medical doctors, chiropractors and naturopaths. Rockefeller got rid of his competition and this is why, to this day, so few states ''recognize'' homeopathy and naturopathy, why no state bureaucracy ''accepts'' natural therapies, and also this is why the chiropractic profession continues to be denigrated by the Establishment.

Rockefeller now more than ever controls all medical doctors, associations, ''health'' charities and government regulatory agencies and what passes as ''approved'' medical treatment in the United States and worldwide. You will find in every state and national archive Rockefeller regulations limiting ''approved'' treatment and dietary advice to Rockefeller drugs and processed foods. It is difficult to understand these nightmare bureaucratic regulations for they are deceptive in their language and hidden intent and are herein reworded to make it crystal clear to help you understand what Rockefeller has in store for you when you go to a Rockefeller oriented orthodox medical doctor.

Every licensed medical doctor is forced to bend his knee or lose his job with the Rockefeller medical Establishment as a result of medical regulations in all 50 states which say one thing but mean the following. Rockefeller drugs and vaccines manufactured in the Rockefeller drug industry are the approved treatment of choice for all disease and if any medical doctor does not prescribe Rockefeller drugs and vaccines as treatment of first choice and does not recommend Rockefeller processed foods, the doctor is practicing outside the scope of his license and risks losing his license to practice Rockefeller medicine.

This means, in effect, that all alternative medical doctors, chiropractors, homeopaths, naturopaths, nutritionists and herbalists, who refuse to compromise themselves to the Rockefeller medical monopoly are quacks, so they say, and their natural non-drug therapies are quackery and outlawed not because they are not effective but only because they are not part of the reprobate Rockefeller medical Establishment.

As a result of this pervasive medical conspiracy, Mullins writes, ''The practice of medicine may not be the world's oldest profession (prostitution), but it is often seen to be operating on much the same principles.''

Mullins says, ''Under the leadership of the nation's two most notorious (Rockefeller) quacks, Simmons and Fishbein (directors of the American Medical Association), a gigantic nationwide drug operation was perfected . . . Today, we suffer from a host of debilitating ailments, both mental and physical, nearly all of which can be traced directly to the operations of the chemical and drug monopoly, and which pose the greatest threat to our continued existence as a nation.''

He continues, ''One physician, Dr. Henry R. Bybee, of Norfolk, Virginia, has publicly stated, ''My honest opinion is that vaccine is the cause of more disease and suffering than anything I could name. I believe that such diseases as cancer, syphilis, cold sores and many other disease conditions are the direct results of vaccination. Yet, in the state of Virginia, and in many other states, parents are compelled to submit their children to this procedure while the medical profession not only receives its pay for this service, but also makes splendid and prospective patients for the future.''

''In medicine,'' says Mullins, ''the Rockefeller influence remains entrenched in its Medical Monopoly. We have mentioned its control of the cancer industry through the Sloan Kettering Cancer Center. We have listed the directors of the major drug firms, each with its director from Chase Manhattan Bank, the Standard Oil Company or other Rockefeller firms. The American College of Surgeons maintains a monopolistic control of hospitals through the powerful Hospital Survey Committee, with members Winthrop Aldrich and David McAlpine representing the Rockefeller control.''

Griffin states, ''FDA spokesmen are the biggest quacks the world has ever seen and it's about time that the American people began to recognize them as such . . . Here, again, we find the classic pattern of government bureaucratic power being used, not for the protection of the people as is its excuse for being, but for the aggrandizement of individuals holding that power and for the elimination of honest competition in the market place . . . Once it (our government) invades the market place and attempts to redistribute the nation's wealth or resources, inevitably it falls into the hands of those who will use it for 'legalized plunder.''

Best selling author, the late Dr. Robert Mendelsohn, M.D. in *Dissent in Medicine* refutes the "science" touted by the orthodox medical Establishment, writing, "The most dangerous form of cancer quackery today is that which is inside modern medicine . . . For example, no form of cancer chemotherapy has ever been subjected to controlled scientific study, that is, in which half the candidates for therapy receive the treatment and the other half do not. . . . The only proven factor in orthodox therapies are the adverse reactions."

In his other books and lectures, Dr. Mendelsohn claims that 95% of all prescribed and over the counter drugs are unproven and ineffective drugs never tested scientifically with controlled studies on humans. So much for modern medical "science"!

Rockefeller has his favorite stars; they include the medical specialists at the very "best" medical institutions, the most successful fund raisers in the Rockefeller "health" charities, the most dishonest propagandists in the Rockefeller controlled media, and Hollywood stars who like to be in the spotlight.

The "top" Rockefeller medical specialists are in a position of trust to do the most damage because the average patient complies without question but never underestimate the damage done by the average orthodox doctor who also pushes Rockefeller drugs. If the "best" specialist recommends by-pass surgery, for example, and then a Hollywood star gives testimony promoting by-pass, you trust them and never mind three major studies proving that by-pass surgery does not prolong life, is counterproductive and is done only because by-pass surgery is the most profitable procedure available and it keeps patients away from natural therapies and wellness.

Rockefeller owns most of the health insurance companies, and you can now understand why "your" health insurance company does not pay for intravenous chelation but only pays for "approved" orthodox diagnosis and treatment, such as by-pass surgery, which costs much more and doesn't even work.

Orthodox medical doctors routinely misdiagnose and mistreat allergy, candidiasis, chronic fatigue syndrome, constipation, free radical pathology, hypothyroidism, systemic toxicity and other common underlying metabolic disorders but alternative medical doctors, nutritional chiropractors and naturopaths effectively and successfully diagnose and treat these basic health problems with natural therapies.

A patient came to me for treatment of chronic low back pain. Faye had a history of pelvic inflammatory disease and ovary-uterus-vaginal problems and my palpation examination showed inflammation, congestion and pain in all of the abdominal area, which is evidence of bowel toxicity. Chiropractic treatments helped but the low back stiffness and pain would return. I advised her that an allergy to wheat often causes female problems because the wheat gluten is almost indigestible, accumulates in the colon and toxifies the whole area including the sexual organs.

Faye said, "I have had this problem for years, even had an exploratory abdominal surgery and my allergy doctor tested me for allergy to pollen, dust, cat dander, etc. but not to wheat and other foods." Since I had heard this type of story about allergy specialists many times before, I told her that orthodox allergy doctors test all the obvious environmental allergens but do not adequately test for common food allergies.

I explained to Faye that alternative medical doctors called clinical ecologists always test food allergy first because they know that when allergenic foods, such as wheat, are removed from the diet, the immune system gets stronger, making her far more tolerant of the environmental allergens. Furthermore, clinical ecologists, nutritional chiropractors and naturopaths will also insist on testing and treating any underlying candidiasis, hypothyroidism, low stomach acid, inadequate pancreatic enzymes, parasites, intestinal infections and other metabolic disorders which make allergy worse. Within two weeks after Faye eliminated wheat from her diet, she recovered from the female problems and her low back stiffness and pain which had bothered her for many years.

The orthodox doctor usually drops the ball when dealing with allergy and his track record with candidiasis is about as poor. Numerous patients have told me that previous testing for candidiasis was negative or that they used to have the problem. They were intrigued when I told them that the orthodox fecal test is non-specific for candidiasis, grossly inaccurate and usually shows up negative when in fact, you may have a very bad case of candidiasis; and that candidiasis is typically a chronic problem and may need to be treated every six months indefinitely.

Epstein-Barr virus or chronic fatigue syndrome, like candidiasis, tends to return again and again and needs intense treatment during active episodes and requires a diligent wellness lifestyle all the time to keep it in check. This is exactly what I told Jeff, a patient with chronic fatigue syndrome. He complained that his orthodox medical doctor gave him antibiotics and a series of tests and was not quite sure if he had Epstein-Barr virus or not. Jeff felt that he was not getting any better and was not able to work for more than an hour at a time.

When Jeff came to me for chiropractic treatment, I unraveled the ins and outs of chronic fatigue syndrome when I told him that most victims of this debilitating disease report year after year of orthodox drugs and endless testing with very little results. In two short weeks on the Detox Diet, eliminating allergenic foods and taking natural supplements to kill or control the virus and to build up the immune system, he was feeling better and was able to go back to work full time. When he starts to feel tired and at the first sign of an infection, he comes in for chiropractic adjustments and to fine tune his therapy program. To date, Jeff has not had a major set-back.

If any of my patients tell their orthodox doctors about systemic toxicity and free radical pathology, it gets to be a pretty confusing and painful experience because I advise them that toxicity and free radicals cause most health problems but their Establishment doctor says that quack doctors propagate these quack theories and only hypochondriacs take them seriously. Strange though, my patients who correct their diets, eliminate toxic foods and bad habits, complete a good bowel cleansing program of detoxification and take free radical scavenger supplements always seem to get well quickly and if a good quack theory really works after all, why not buy it?

Dr. Broda Barnes' basal temperature test for hypothyroidism is another of those quack theories that works. Dr. Barnes after forty years of experience testing patients for hypothyroidism found that the resting basal temperature effectively tests the function of the thyroid gland but that ordinary blood thyroid tests for the presence of thyroid hormone are not accurate or reliable and typically show no problem when you actually have a low thyroid problem, which can make you sick in thousands of ways. Now who is right? The orthodox doctor or Dr. Barnes? Hundreds of alternative doctors across the nation say that Dr. Barnes is right and that natural Armour thyroid is far more effective than the synthetics pushed by Establishment doctors.

When you look at what is going on with allergy, candidiasis, chronic fatigue syndrome, toxicity, free radical pathology, hypothyroidism and other underlying metabolic disorders, you can safely say that orthodox medical doctors don't think much of them and that alternative doctors don't think much of the orthodox doctors' mismanagement of metabolic problems.

In cancer treatment, for example, alternative doctors know that the average orthodox doctor: recommends the unhealthful foods and looks the other way concerning bad habits which slowly but surely cause the underlying metabolic disorders, when left untreated are the true cause of cancer and other degenerative diseases; treats mere symptoms not causes of health problems with Rockefeller drugs allowing the cancer to develop and take hold of your body; uses diagnostics that are too crude to pick up cancer in the early stages; then when the cancer is fully developed and when it is almost too late to do much about it, the ineffective cancer drugs and other approved Rockefeller therapies are used and usually make the cancer patient worse; proven alternative cancer therapies, like intravenous chelation, laetrile, ozone therapy, hyperbaric oxygen, oxygen during exercise, photoluminescence, immune system enhancement and enzymes are discouraged because Rockefeller does not profit from them; the average cancer patient under orthodox care dies unnecessarily; the Establishment doctor claims that he did his best; the average family of the cancer victim simply accepts this as fact on face value and ironically may donate money for orthodox cancer research which has only increased the cancer death rate despite misleading claims to the contrary.

Aren't you hearing more and more about cancer and AIDS patients who simply choose to die and do not seriously consider the possible benefits of chelation and ozone therapy and all the other effective alternative therapies used successfully in Germany for the past fifty years by patients who choose not to die?

Burn this into your hearts, minds and spirits: Cancer, arthritis, heart disease, AIDS and other degenerative diseases cannot be treated effectively until the unhealthful diet, bad habits and underlying metabolic disorders, namely, toxicity, free radical pathology, allergy, hypothyroidism, hiatal hernia, candidiasis, chronic fatigue syndrome, etc. have been identified and corrected and your alternative doctor can help. At some point, any objective person is compelled to ask, "Do orthodox medical doctors intentionally mismanage underlying metabolic disorders, thereby allowing your body to break down and develop cancer, cardiovascular disease, arthritis and other degenerative diseases?"

Protect yourself and those you love by learning more about the medical Establishment. You don't have to be sick, tired, overweight or depressed. You don't have to accept second rate orthodox health care. You don't have to be zonked out on drugs that you likely don't need anyway. You may not need surgery in that about 80% of elective surgery is not necessary. You may be suffering unknowingly from a simple underlying metabolic disorder which can be easily corrected.

WELLNESS DOCTORS AND ALTERNATIVE THERAPIES

Find a good alternative wellness medical doctor, chiropractor or naturopath who treats the whole person with a complete program of detoxification and natural therapies to heal your body and build up your immune system. If you need a specialist, perhaps he can refer you to an alternative specialist. It is especially important to establish a relationship with a good doctor in case of emergencies when you might not have time to be too selective.

You owe it to yourself to be healthy, happy, energetic and slender. Why not have the best doctor and the best that life has to offer?

I would like to share with you a few quotes from happy guests at our Dr. Deal's Hawaiian Wellness Holiday here on Kauai, the Garden Island of Hawaii. My wife Roberleigh and I advertise in health magazines and bring guests over for a wellness vacation of yoga, aerobics, aquacise, scenic walks and hikes, excursions to secret beaches, delicious Detox Diet or slim down meals, nutritional guidance, weight loss, natural therapies, massage and chiropractic.

"Most of our health problems have completely disappeared. My mom, dad, grandma and grandpa have all lost 6 to 7 pounds on the cleansing diet in one week. And everyone is feeling very well."   — The Lubker Family, Boulder, Colo.

"I've felt better this past week than I've felt in years."
— Marie Foy, Charlotte, N.C.

"Thank you for your tender loving care. I am a new woman."
— Christine De Lange, New York City

"Now that I follow Dr. Deal's recommendations, my health is radically improved and I don't get sick anymore."
— Thomas Willcox, Philadelphia, Pa.
"I had such a wonderful healing time. Keep on doing what you are doing — it's a great gift!"
— Roberta Wagner, Washington, D.C.

Now a list of wellness doctors and organizations around the country:

Cancer Control Society, 2043 N. Berendo St., Los Angeles, California 90027, telephone (213) 663-7801 for a list of alternative doctors for all health problems and diseases. The Cancer Control Society has the best and most well rounded list of alternative therapies available in America and the world. Join, contribute and start a local chapter in your community.

American College of Advancement in Medicine, 23121 Verdugo Drive, Suite 204, Laguna Hills, California 92653, telephone (714) 583-7666 to request the name, address and telephone number of an alternative wellness medical doctor or osteopath in your area who does intravenous chelation and other natural therapies. Order the current membership roster (there is a charge of $8) for the United States to refer your family and friends in other states.

National Health Federation, P.O. Box 688, Monrovia, California 91016, telephone (818) 357-2181 to request a referral to an alternative wellness medical doctor, chiropractor or naturopath nearest you. Join the NHF ($36) to receive Health Freedom News magazine monthly and to help protect your freedom of choice regarding your health.

Dr. William Campbell Douglass, M.D., Photobiology Treatment Center, P.O. Box 888, Clayton, GA 30525, telephone (404) 782-7222. Send $3 for a brochure explaining the use of photoluminescence, chelation, bio-oxidation, exercise with oxygen therapy, etc. for cancer, hepatitis, diabetes, chronic fatigue syndrome, cardiovascular disease, AIDS and other diseases.

Lanny Smith, Ultra Life, Inc., P.O. Box 440 Dept M, Carlyle, Ill. 62231, telephone (800) 323-3842 or (618) 594-7711. Send $5 for the ozone and hydrogen peroxide information pack. Also contact Living Wellness, P.O. Box 279, Koloa, HI 96756, telephone (800) 338-6977 or (808) 332-9244.

Dr. Agatha Thrash, M.D., Uchee Pines Institute, Route 1,

Box 443, Seale, Alabama 36875-9124, telephone (205) 855-4764. Dr. Thrash is a Seventh Day Adventist health reformer who ministers to the physical, mental and spiritual needs through the methods presented in the Bible and the writings of Ellen G. White.

International Bio-oxidative Medicine Foundation, P.O. Box 61767, Dallas/Ft. Worth, Texas 75261 for a referral to the closest medical doctor using ozone and intravenous hydrogen peroxide.

Educational Concerns for Hydrogen and Oxygen, P.O. Box 126, Delano, Minnesota 55328. Send a $5 donation and request information on ozone and hydrogen peroxide.

Reams Biological Theory of Ionization therapy is available from Dr. Joseph Mathei, D.C., 853 Scotland Road, Quarryville, PA 17566, telephone (707) 284-3181 or Dr. June Wiles, Holistic Laboratories, 5025 E. Fowler Avenue, #13, Tampa, Florida 33617, telephone (813) 988-7788. The Reams method measures saliva and urine acid-alkaline pH, blood sugar, etc. and recommends foods and supplements to balance the body providing effective results for many difficult health problems.

Dr. N.W. Boyd, D.O., Boyd Clinic, Loganville, PA 17342, telephone (717) 428-2436. Dr. Boyd uses injectable sclerosing (scarring) agents to strengthen weak areas, hernias, rectal and prostate problems. Order his book *How to Stay out of the Hospital* $6.

American Association of Acupuncture and Bio-Energetic Medicine, 1270 Queen Emma St., Suite 501, Honolulu, Hawaii 96813, telephone (808) 537-3311 or 235-2452 to ask for a referral to the nearest doctor who uses Computron, Interro or Listen electrodiagnosis and treatment, which can pick up and treat very subtle allergies and health problems in the early stages.

World Research Foundation, 15300 Ventura Blvd., Suite 405, Sherman Oaks, CA 91403, telephone (818) 907-5483. Books, tapes and referrals to alternative doctors in America and all over the world who use the latest alternative therapies.

International Medical Center, 424 Executive Center Blvd. Suite 100, El Paso, TX 79902, telephone (800) 621-8924 or (915) 534-0272 founded by the late Dr. Ray Evers, the father of alternative wellness medicine who coined the word "holistic" medicine. The clinic has a variety of alternative therapies and Dr. Evers' own patented non-toxic chelating agent and treats cardiovascular disease, cancer, arthritis and other degenerative diseases.

Hospital Santa Monica, 424 Calle Primera #102, San Ysidro, California 92073, telephone (619) 428-1146. Dr. Kurt Donsbach, Ph.D., D.C. and his staff of wellness medical doctors and chiropractors treat all acute and chronic diseases with the latest alternative therapies. Order a free catalog for therapies by mail to treat cancer, arthritis, cardiovascular disease and other metabolic illnesses.

Dr. Jaime Narvaez, M.D., Care of: Nadine Rogers, P.O. Box 241, Booneville, Arkansas 72927, telephone (800) 862-5551 or (501) 675-4962. Dr. Narvaez was with the former Manner Metabolic Clinic founded by the late Dr. Harold Manner, Ph.D., author of *The End of Cancer*. Dr. Narvaez treats cancer, arthritis, multiple sclerosis and all diseases with the Manner metabolic therapy in his clinic in Juarez, Mexico and you can call him directly at 011-521-613-2975 or call Nadine at the above numbers.

Teri and Lindsey Williams to order a copy of their book *You Can Live* for $8.50, P.O. Box 17542, Scottsdale, AZ 85269 as a referral guide to natural health centers and health products in America and Mexico.

VitaChem International, 241 Hazel Avenue, Redwood City, CA 94061, telephone (800) 227-8823 or (415) 365-6692 for apricot seeds and amygdalin (laetrile) extracted from apricot seeds. VitaChem recommends 10 apricot seeds a day to prevent cancer.

RECOMMENDED READING

A Textbook of Natural Medicine by naturopathic Drs. Joseph Pizzorno and Michael Murray, N.D., $325 (worth it), Bastyr Naturopathic College, 144 N.E. 54th, Seattle, WA 98105, telephone (206) 523-9585. This naturopathic textbook is the collected works of Drs. Pizzorno, Murray and other contributors, represents the primary textbook used in the four year naturopathic college curriculum and covers most of the natural therapies for common health problems. It may well be the most important and practical book on natural therapy that any alternative medical doctor, chiropractor or naturopath uses in his practice of natural medicine. This excellent text should be used as a model and prototype to replace most if not all fragmented orthodox medical texts used in all medical, chiropractic and naturopathic schools. Also recommended for the general public and a shorter version is available in paperback for $21.95 entitled *Encyclopedia of Natural Medicine* from Vital Communications, 12819 S.E. 38th St., Suite 159, Bellevue, WA 98006, telephone (800) 488-0753.

Purchase or order from your bookstore *Fit For Life* by Harvey and Marilyn Diamond and also their book *Fit For Life II* which so graciously recommends Dr. Deal's Hawaiian Wellness Holiday. Their first book outlines the Fit For Life diet and their second book details the politics of orthodox medicine and Establishment nutrition and also provides a program of good health care.

Order *Eat For Strength Oil Free: A Vegetarian Cookbook* and also *Home Remedies* and *Charcoal* by Drs. Agatha and Calvin Thrash, M.D. from Uchee Pines Health Conditioning Center, Route 1, Box 273, Seale, AL 36875, telephone (205) 855-4764.

Order *Murder By Injection* by Eustace Mullins from Mr. Mullins, P.O. Box 1105, Staunton, Virginia 24401 to understand the politics of the orthodox Rockefeller medical Establishment. Also order his other books, *The Rape of Justice*, *Secrets of the Federal Reserve*, *The World Order*, $20 each.

Order *World Without Cancer* by G. Edward Griffin, American Media, Box 4646, Westlake Village, CA 91359, telephone (800) 282-2873. A classic expose of the Rockefeller medical monopoly and how it controls the orthodox cancer industry, book $12, audio tape $11, *Politics of Cancer Therapy* audio tape $11. Request list of books and tapes, especially *The Grand Design* audio tape $12, video tape $35 to help you understand the plans Bush, Rockefeller and other internationalists have in store for us.

Contact the new Christian Crusade Church, P.O. Box 426, Metairie, LA 70004, telephone (800) 882-9199. Request a list of books and tapes documenting the internationalists' conspiracy against America.

Write the Institute of Historical Review, 1822½ Newport Blvd., Suite 191, Costa Mesa, CA 92627 to request catalog of books and tapes presenting the true history of America and the world and our common enemies who masquerade as allies.

Write for a list of audio tapes of sermons by Pastor Conrad Jarrell by writing to John Damico, 745 Helmhill Ave., Las Vegas, Nevada 89123, telephone (702) 897-7726 to see what you might be missing in your church.

Subscribe to the Spotlight (national weekly newspaper), 300 Independence Ave., S.E., Washington, D.C. 20003, telephone

(800) 522-6292 or (202) 546-5621 and request airmail delivery to get the real news quickly.

Also from your bookstore, purchase or order *Medical Heretic* and also *How to Raise a Healthy Child in Spite of Your Doctor* by Robert Mendelsohn, M.D.: *Colon Health* by Norman Walker, Ph.D.; *Everywoman's Book* by Paavo Airola, Ph.D.; *Hypothyroidism* by Broda Barnes, M.D.; *The Yeast Connection* by William Crook, M.D.; *Bypassing Bypass* (chelation therapy) by Elmer Cranton, M.D.; and *Oxygen Therapies* by Ed McCabe.

WELLNESS PRAYER AND AFFIRMATION:

I ,_____YOUR NAME_____ , pray and affirm to God on this day that I am beginning a new life with radiant health. I am discarding from my body, mind and heart all negative conditioning and releasing all of it into the hands of God for His help and His way as my way.

I forgive myself and I forgive those who have hurt, disappointed or wronged me as I am forgiven in Him.

I am God's child and He has bestowed in me infinite possibilities; nothing is impossible for Almighty God or for me in Him.

I am now free of the world and free of my own limitations, fears and worries and I now welcome joy, love, compassion, understanding, wholesome food, natural therapies and wellness in my life.

I feel better and healthier every day and it feels so good and so right and I give daily thanks to God and pray that He blesses me with wellness in every way.

INDEX

ORDER

Dr. Deal's Delicious Detox Diet, Weight Loss, Wellness Lifestyle. Get a copy for a family member or friend. $16 plus $4 shipping.

Dr. Deal's Holistic Chiropractic Protocol. Learn bodywork to diagnose how unhealthful foods and habits cause congestion in liver, intestines, kidneys, etc. leading to neck and back stiffness and pain and health problems. Monograph. $10 plus $4 shipping.

Dr. Deal's Hawaiian Wellness Holiday. Shape up, slim down and create a wellness lifestyle on the Garden Island of Kauai. Yoga, aerobics, aquacize, walks, hikes, massage, chiropractic, natural therapies, delicious meals. Call (800) 338-6977 for brochure.

Dr. Deal's Hawaiian Face, Body and Massage Lotion. Creamy and wonderful! Aloe, coconut oil, herbs. 8 oz., Ginger Blossom, Plumeria or Herbal. $10 plus $4 shipping.

Dr. Deal's Upright Colonic. Self-administered in sitting position on toilet. Includes colonic, 5 gal. bag, shower water diverter, fill-up hose, tubing, pencil-thin rectal tips, instructions. Rolls up into 6 by 15 inches for travel. Helps you feel good about yourself and humanity! $150 plus $10 shipping.

Inquire about water distillers and filters, shower water filters; ozone air purification machines; herbs, silymarin and ginkgo concentrates, minerals, thymus tablets, oral chelation tablets, Dr. Donsbach's Super Oxy Aloe Tonic with hydrogen peroxide, and more.

LIVING WELLNESS
Dr. Grady A. Deal, Ph.D., D.C.
P.O. Box 279
Koloa, Kauai, Hawaii 96756
(800) 338-6977